What people are saying about
Education Revolution

Sam Shain's book addresses and boldly answers a burning question for our time: how to develop critical political awareness given corporate media and their political biases. As a public high-school teacher, he has long practiced answers to the question. This book contains the wisdom he has acquired. He tells us what needs to be taught and how to generate media literacy. The US left especially needs to read this as an important source for changing the major narratives through which people today make sense of a capitalism in crisis.

Richard Wolff, author of *Democracy At Work*, host of *Economic Update* podcast

We live in a deeply unjust and unequal society. High school students are bombarded with propaganda to justify the status quo, from the reassuring fairy tales about capitalism in their economics classes to textbooks in their US History classes that are splattered with more pictures of eagles and slowly waving flags than the signs at a Trump rally. Sam Shain understands how important it is to equip these students with the reasoning tools they can use to think for themselves and see through all the nonsense. We need about 10,000 more of him.

Ben Burgis, author of *Canceling Comedians While the World Burns: A Critique of the Contemporary Left*

High school students' anonymous reviews on Mr Shain's journalism class

As a liberal and left thinking person, Mr Shain's journalism class has helped me become more open-minded in talking with my Trump supporting father.

I learned a lot about how the world actually operates around me. We are all sort of blinded to this idea of reality, and during this class I was like un-blinded I guess? I don't know what words to use exactly, but I was really shown how the world does work and how I can become its pawn or work against it.

I learned that you must view everything with an open mind and not let one article guide your opinion.

I learned so much about viewing the world, especially mass media, through a critical eye this year. I learned about what traps we fall into while viewing media and how we can prevent that. I also learned about good vs. questionable journalism tactics and how this can affect how accurate a news source is.

I think all of the discussions on the working world and capitalism will be useful for me when I enter the working world.

I've become more open-minded.

I think more deeply.

Education Revolution

Media Literacy for Political Awareness

Education Revolution

Media Literacy for Political Awareness

Sam Shain

Winchester, UK
Washington, USA

JOHN HUNT PUBLISHING

First published by Zero Books, 2022
Zero Books is an imprint of John Hunt Publishing Ltd., No. 3 East St., Alresford,
Hampshire SO24 9EE, UK
office@jhpbooks.com
www.johnhuntpublishing.com
www.zero-books.net

For distributor details and how to order please visit the 'Ordering' section on our website.

ISBN: 978 1 78535 311 6
978 1 78535 361 1 (ebook)
Library of Congress Control Number: 2021942965

A CIP catalogue record for this book is available from the British Library.

Design: Stuart Davies

UK: Printed and bound by CPI Group (UK) Ltd, Croydon, CR0 4YY
Printed in North America by CPI GPS partners

We operate a distinctive and ethical publishing philosophy in
all areas of our business, from our global network of authors to
production and worldwide distribution.

Contents

To my baby son, Sonder. May the world become a better place for him and his generation, their children, and all future generations around the world.

"[Edward Bernays] (the father of public relations) writes, 'those who manipulate this unseen mechanism of society constitute an invisible government which is the true ruling power of our country. We are governed, our minds molded, our tastes formed, our ideas suggested, largely by men we have never heard of.' This might sound like the ramblings of a conspiracy theorist, but in fact it is far more nefarious: it is an invitation to the conspiracy, drafted by one of its founding fathers, and targeted to would-be titans of industry who would like to have a seat on his shadow council of thought leaders.

Perhaps Bernays overstated his case, but his ideas have troubling consequences. If he is right, then the very idea of a democratic society is a chimera: the will of the people is something to be shaped by hidden powers, making representative government meaningless. Our only hope is to identify the tools by which our beliefs, opinions, and preferences are shaped, and look for ways to re-exert control."

The Misinformation Age by Cailin O'Connor and James Owen Weatherall

Author's Note

As I point out in this book, *America's place on the political spectrum is objectively right wing*. America is an individualized, increasingly privatized, and corporatized society. America has campaign funding laws that allow massive amounts of private special interest money to dominate the political process. We have a corporate media that carries the veneer of independence, but is ultimately more interested in preserving power and gaining profit than informing the populace and daring to be adversarial to power. We have private corporate power that essentially does whatever it wants. When I talk about "the Right" and "the Left" in this book, I am not talking about "Republicans" and "Democrats" respectively. Rather, I am talking about liberalism, which emphasizes the individual and personal responsibility, and socialism, which emphasizes broader systems and structures. Or if you'd rather, capitalists and working class, or private and public sector, respectively.

In this book, when I say "The Right," I am generally talking about people and entities who believe in authoritarianism, privatization, corporatism, individualism, the "free market," "trickle-down economics," American exceptionalism/nationalism, and do not actually believe in democracy; but rather more or less in preserving and further compounding power where it already exists – a goal which naturally requires a substantial disinformation campaign.

When I talk about "The Left" I am discussing people who believe in shifting power from the private and corporate sector into the hands of the working class, or even an elected government to some degree. I am talking about working-class people who believe in free speech, a robust public sector (including education, of course), civil liberties, and know and understand the clear and present danger economically, environmentally, and authoritatively of capitalism as a system.

With these definitions in mind, I would argue that both American political parties are on "the Right." The GOP is increasingly far right, and Democrats like Joe Biden, Hillary Clinton, or Barack Obama, who agree with the GOP on imperialist foreign policy, military and police spending, corporate tax breaks and subsidies, capitalism in general, are not too strikingly different if you put aside the disingenuous rhetoric and take an honest look at their voting records and policies.

If you ask the average working-class person how they feel about taxing multinational corporations and billionaires or how we run healthcare, for examples, most are going to agree they should be taxed at a higher rate and healthcare shouldn't operate for profit, respectively. "The Left" is a much broader bloc of people than we tend to think, especially if the issues are simply presented fairly, free from manipulative framing.

And it would be even larger if we taught people in schools how to see beyond narratives peddled by the powerful, and be knowledgeable and skeptical enough to know, understand, and act upon their own interests.

Ultimately, this book is about using public schools to help the common person gain more power in this country.

Part One

The Basics of Journalism

Introduction

I used to be Facebook friends with a high school classmate (we'll call him Trevor) who really hated teachers. Sure, he'd never come out and say, "I hate teachers," but he thought public schools should be abolished. He thought we were overpaid and essentially welfare recipients who didn't really contribute anything to humanity. He thought we were a general waste of space. He always said he planned to homeschool his kids because teachers were such losers, and he wanted to avoid the supposed "liberal indoctrination" of youths provided by our public school system. I would argue this is not only a slight to teachers but the idea of education and knowledge itself.

The reason certain people like Trevor end up feeling this way about teachers (which is of course always accompanied by the typical stew of insane beliefs – climate science is a hoax, our country is somehow post-racial because Obama, or COVID-19 was nothing more than a "Plandemic") is because of the rapid spread of disinformation and brutally simplistic messaging by powerful and wealthy right-wing media platforms within a country in which both major parties continue to drift rightward (both economically and authoritatively) year after year. It's because our entire culture has been propagandized by our corporate media and politicians to believe that our economy is a law of nature, thereby meaning if someone is rich it's because they worked incredibly hard, or if someone is poor it's because they are lazy. There is no nuance, no acknowledgment of history or systems, just mindless individualism. This type of attitude is required if sense is to be made of this insane system. Trevor didn't know how to critically think beyond the rhetoric of Fox News or the so-called "Intellectual Dark Web" (as dubbed by the *New York Times,* right-wing internet stars like Ben Shapiro, Jordan Peterson, Dave Rubin, etc.) watered down version of the world. Guys like Trevor find a simple answer that makes them feel correct and persecuted, feeling emboldened to pass along what they learned from these hacks, spreading the grift like a virus to their own detriment.

Don't get me wrong, even though I fancy myself as an intelligent skeptic when it comes to media consumption, I have a hard time dealing with the information onslaught – anyone would. But the reason this guy and I grew up together and have such opposing views, not only of our former high school but of the world in general, isn't because he was able to escape some public school liberal indoctrination machine, I would argue the exact opposite: the public school system didn't do well enough in preparing him to think about how to sift through information or think about positioning himself in a place politically that would be advantageous to his own self-interests. I know this because, though I did have plenty of wonderful and informative teachers, in this particular respect it didn't do well enough in teaching me how to be more politically aware of my own interests as a working-class person either. I had to do it on my own, just as Trevor did, but we each took incredibly different paths based on what type of content we encountered later in life, or how we were raised. Throughout this book I will tackle a lot of the points made by the right-wing "Intellectual Dark Web" types, the messaging by right-wing corporate media (spoiler: this includes liberal favorites like the *NY Times*), as well as unfounded, baseless disinformation that comes in so many forms in the age of the internet. I wish their rhetoric could be written off as inconsequential, rendering further analysis of their drivel within this text a waste of time, but frankly the existence of these outlets and their unfortunately massive influence is a huge reason why my curriculum and this book should be taken seriously and read widely immediately.

People don't know what they don't know. Without an honest look at politics, everything is just assumed to be the way it is as a natural law with no other alternative. Without a legitimate critique of the powerful, people start to blame nonsense like "RussiaGate" or the "cancelation" of Dr Seuss or Mr Potatohead for their problems rather than taking aim at the corporations, and their toady politicians, that are truly oppressing and exploiting them. The foolhardy culture wars and conspiracy theories persist on both sides, I believe, because those are far easier to grasp than a thoughtful, intelligent, and legitimate critique of power in this country with solutions that would actually benefit the working class such as workers' rights, unionization, and a robust public sector. Furthermore, corporate media, with all of their wealth and power, would rather emphasize those issues than true working-class grievances.

Why should public schools be expected to teach anything but a left-leaning version of current events and history, anyway? Should I, a teacher making a living off of a public institution, really encourage right-wing privatization? Should I be teaching winner-take-all capitalism? Disaster capitalism? How would it make sense for a teacher working in the public sector to teach the merits of privatization? If questions about healthcare come up, should I not tell them the truth about how it would cost me $14,000 (in a healthy year) to insure my wife and son while under a single-payer plan it would cost $500-$1000? We have seen winner-take-all capitalism enriches a handful of winners with wealth they could never spend in multiple lifetimes while four in five Americans live paycheck to paycheck. Is telling these truths out of line because "politics"? Why is there the existing stigma that "politics" has no place in the classroom, anyway? As teachers, perhaps it's time to rethink not only the content in our classrooms, but the way the country itself is structured if so many of our students are destined to struggle with the problems of wealth inequality, student debt, the climate crisis, and a host of other issues within late-stage capitalism.

Of course, some readers are thinking, "yeah so don't teach this sort of material at all – politics doesn't belong in the classroom," or, "students shouldn't know a teacher's political beliefs." These are inherently right-wing positions. Avoiding these topics, pretending they don't exist, not only isn't fooling high school students, but also marginalizes and disregards existing issues in the world and attempts to impede progress by maintaining the status quo. If we don't begin to discuss these things more often in schools, as I will argue through a working-person's lens since most kids are going to earn their living using their labor, not their capital investments, then they are subject to other forces on their own to develop a sense of how the world works. These forces too often are those with the deepest pockets, including our corporatized media, our corporatized political parties, our corporatized TV networks, and our vast and confusing internet filled with faux-intellectual grifters, funded by giant industries, who sound so convincing without a worthy opponent to push back on the lies they are spewing. Schools must provide a space to confront this disinformation head on.

When it's framed in this fashion, how could it be seen as dangerous for kids to begin thinking about this stuff with guidance and at an earlier age? Perhaps, for example, if the human-caused element of the climate crisis had been taught as a foregone conclusion and the forces of greed in the corporate sector weren't able to prey on an ignorant populace by swooping in and spinning absurdities regarding the issue, this country would have done something about it a long time ago.

We're living through a time when conspiracy theories aren't just rarely-discussed fringe ideas, or relegated to the depths of the internet, they're actually shaping public policy, or lack thereof, in real time. During COVID-19 Americans were banned from traveling to the European Union because we've allowed the ideology of "Plandemic," an internet video claiming all sorts of outrageous nonsense about COVID-19, insinuating the whole thing is a hoax, to guide COVID-19 response policy, which has largely amounted to doing absolutely nothing at all and going back to what Americans perceive as "normal" because we lack any sort of imagination to conjure up a meaningful alternative. We saw millions of people after the 2020 presidential election accept the baseless premise that the election was "fraudulent" – not because evidence existed to prove this claim, but because that's what they wanted to hear. So horrendous is America at critical thinking that *The Economist* and *YouGov* discovered in polling that over 80 percent of Trump's voters believe the devoid-of-evidence claims he made after the 2020 election. In a Zoom journalism class during COVID, merely pointing out that Trump's actions were unprecedented and his claims completely unfounded left a parent feeling obliged and emboldened to invade my class and claim I was "just giving my opinion" to the students. When I calmly asked him to simply relay any evidence of Trump's claims, just before he claimed 2020 was the same as the 2000 election (not even close if you simply look at the numbers), he had very little to say. Frankly, I believe he would not have felt emboldened to do that, or would not have been tricked into believing the words of one lying politician over objective reality in the first place, had he taken a class like mine in high school.

We're witnessing large numbers of people earnestly believing that we are in a post-racial society because our sense of history, in their minds, lives and dies with whether or not Confederate statues remain standing rather than substantial knowledge of different periods of time. On the other side, far too many people are satisfied with empty gestures like painting slogans on a street (or removing Confederate statues for that matter) rather than actual systemic change occurring to curtail existing issues – and perhaps the reason some are pacified by this is because they've never been introduced to the problems, let alone some ideas for solutions.

In 2020 the "choice" for president was the authoritarian-curious incumbent Donald Trump versus the author of the "tough on crime" bill, who also voted for the Iraq War and has spent a career as a pawn for corporate interests, Joe Biden. Both men have been accused of sexual assault, both were quoted in mainstream publications discussing how they would fare in a fight against the other, and they even floated a push-up contest. This is clearly not the choice that an educated, thoughtful populace would wind up with in any rational world. The right and the so-called "left" arguing about who is tougher on crime, for decades now within a country which puts more people in cages than anywhere else on the planet (America is home to nearly 25 percent of the *world's* prison population), should truly be a cause of concern.

Incidentally, it seems it is through the avenue of criticizing "both sides" over a set of moral principles such as anti-war, equality, civil rights, and preservation of our environment that a teacher can avoid partisanship because neither party at this point in time has done a very good job on a variety of these issues. This is not to say that both parties are equally bad, or one is better than the other, I think it's more complex than that, but it does give teachers the ability to relieve any angsty parents in being able to say, "this class is political, as nearly everything is these days, but most certainly not *partisan*." None of my classes are partisan because I would never preach to kids to specifically vote for a certain party or candidate, but it is political in that we discuss politics, current events, and current issues, because I am trying to make my classes relevant and meaningful. If a movement arises to stifle that sort of discussion in the classroom, I think we'd have yet another serious problem on our hands.

Though my aim in this book is to give teachers the confidence and arguments to dare to teach this stuff in class, at times it may not be easy and teachers might need to fight for their curriculums. In my third year teaching, my administration, which overall is a true pleasure to work with, floated elimination of the book

Rising Out of Hatred from my freshman English curriculum after a parent complaint. My administration stated the book was "too political" and for a moment considered removal of the text – in their defense, it's a difficult job making everyone happy as an administrator, balancing the happiness of parents, teachers, boards, and students.

Rising Out of Hatred is a book by *Washington Post* journalist Eli Saslow about a reformed white nationalist, Derek Black, who disavows his formerly hateful beliefs by attending New College, a diverse and progressive school. It's a story of love, patience, and inclusion. Some students wanted the former white nationalist banned from New College because he was a young and prominent white nationalist figure, others stuck with him and through their compassion, understanding, and unfathomable patience eventually lifted him out of hate. The book lends itself to wonderful discussions about free speech, race, love, hate, violence, and so much more beyond the seemingly all-encompassing "politics." The idea that this story should be banned on the grounds that it is "too political," to me is blatantly outrageous, but nonetheless, there was a period of pushback before ultimately getting the book reinstated with an option for students to opt-out – which I would say is a fair solution for all involved. To my administration's credit, they were willing to hear my arguments to keep the book alive. The arguments I used in a meeting with administration and the concerned parents in a meeting that year can be found in the pages of this book.

Speaking more broadly now, should material in schools be in jeopardy if a student, parent, or handful of parents complain it's "too political"? It doesn't seem like a wise idea. It seems clear that such complaints could undoubtedly become weaponized. If classroom content is objectively true, how could it possibly be removed? Shouldn't the truth itself be important and healthy for students to know? Particularly when they're in high school and a few short years away from entering the "real world"? Saying otherwise is essentially a glorified version of the tactic of accusing information of being "fake news" just because the recipient of the information doesn't like what it says. One might refer to such an act as "cancel culture." The truth cannot be changed, only obscured. I am a high school English teacher who reads extensively and happens to pay significant attention to the goings on of the world – as I would argue any educator should. It will be doing a great service to future generations to pass along these truths, to expose the problems that plague our country so conditions can continuously improve as time goes on. Though I've barely scratched the surface and continue to learn daily, I have dedicated a huge portion of my life to learning how the world works. While I still have a lot to learn, it seems I should most certainly be able to pass what I have learned along to my students.

But what falls under the umbrella of "politics" and why shouldn't it be allowed in our classrooms, anyway? Literally anything could be deemed "political." Something as basic as wearing masks in public spaces during a global pandemic was somehow politicized in this country. The science regarding human-caused climate change is apparently up for debate because, for big oil, the reality of the situation is so inconvenient for profit an alt-reality must be conjured up. In fact, we constantly see reality itself contorted so it fits nicely into the idea that history has ended, and capitalism is as good as it gets. Are we really supposed to give credence to both the truth and the anti-reality side of things, solely because the right wing has the wealth and resources to put utter nonsense and disinformation out there in the name of preserving profit? Saying "politics cannot be in the classroom" is so vague it could apply to literally anything. Any lesson on class and poverty, a theme touched upon countless times in classic literature, could be deemed as "political" by an angsty right-wing parent who was hell-bent on removing politics from the classroom and by extension maintaining the unsustainable status quo. I call on teachers to teach this material and for administrators to commit to defending it.

In English and History classes, through omission and emphasis, it is not only nearly impossible to avoid "political" concepts, but also impossible not to reveal some level of bias on matters that are subjective and moral rather than objective and scientific. English and history isn't math and science, we are instead often dealing with moral questions. For example, there is no law of nature that indicates we *must* view each other as equals, treat each other with respect, or even avoid a culture of slavery, these are moral conclusions. Morally speaking, it used to be generally acceptable to literally own human beings in this country. The idea that human beings could be owned had to be dismantled not only through a physical battle, but an ideological battle as well, because there was no cut and dry law of nature for abolitionists to point to, there was no scientific conclusion, it was a moral question. We can use facts to back our morals, but at the end of the day we can't exactly prove that everyone must be treated equally and slavery, according to cold hard scientific fact and peer-reviewed studies, must be abolished.

English and history classes must take a moral stance on different topics. When we consider the objective realities of widening inequality, a climate under attack by corporate America, privatized healthcare and higher education looting the incomes of American workers with union membership on the decline and wages stagnant, and the public sector (including our own institutions of schools) increasingly under attack with threats to privatize or stifle certain content, what choice do we have but to educate students about politics and do so from the left? The reason the "no politics in school" rhetoric even exists is to preserve the status quo as the deep pockets of right-wing disinformation manipulate public opinion by bending reality and swaying public consciousness with their half-baked versions of history, civics, political and economic theory, and social issues. We don't give credence to both the Union and the Confederacy (at least not up here in Maine), we rightfully acknowledge that the south's stance was wrong and morally abhorrent. Why should it be any different to point out that the side that constantly strives for widening inequality, destroying the environment for profit, turning profit off of people's health issues, etc. is equally morally repugnant? Just because it's happening in real time and isn't ancient history doesn't mean we shouldn't be discussing these moral questions in classrooms. What kind of world do we want? I happen to be a teacher who knows about a lot of these issues; why shouldn't my students be made aware of them as well as they get ready to act within and inherit this world?

One final point – though on many issues both Democrats and Republicans can be criticized, on others they can't. The Republican Party is demonstrably worse on voting rights, for example. As stated essentially aloud by the party's leaders including Trump, the more people that vote, the less-likely Republican victories are, which means the logical goal in maintaining Republican power is to limit democracy itself. Conservative Justice Brett Kavanaugh literally warned in a ruling leading up to the 2020 election that, "Those States want to avoid the chaos and suspicions of impropriety that can ensue if thousands of absentee ballots flow in after election day and potentially flip the results of an election. And those States also want to be able to definitively announce the results of the election on election night, or as soon as possible thereafter." Read: more people voting would be different than fewer people voting, and fewer people voting is good for the GOP. Though the idea of democracy of course isn't a foregone conclusion, etched in stone in the laws of nature as the indisputably best system based on proven scientific analysis or peer-reviewed studies, it seems like a moral argument worth fighting for in public schools just as is the fight against racism. The fact I can't juxtapose this with an equally ill-fated anti-democracy effort by "the other side," to me, doesn't mean this issue shouldn't be mentioned in classes because, again, voter suppression in this country as outlined by Carol Anderson in *One Person, No Vote* is something that is objectively happening. Yes, my bias leads me to mentioning this in class, and though I avoid partisanship, I don't believe it's even partisan to point out something that is literally happening in our country. The idea we shouldn't say this because "politics" or "call out both sides the same" is absurd because it doesn't change the fact that something is happening, it just inherently obscures the truth. If a school gives a presentation about the dangers of smoking cigarettes or vaping, is it super important to make sure Big Tobacco or the vaping industry get their equal time to come in and give their two cents? Oh, it's a public health risk, you say? The same could be said about a variety of the issues mentioned thus far.

So enter the public school system and its army of teachers. I, for one, am just an average journalist turned high school English teacher. I am a millennial from Maine who went to a small college, graduated in debt up to my eyeballs, worked my first job out of college as a journalist for a measly $11 an hour, got laid off for the first time at age 24, went back to doing manual labor and painting houses with my college degree as I paid off the debt while living at home, got hired back at my newspaper only to lose the job again months later when the paper closed in the post-recession wake, then got my start in education as an Ed Tech at a behavioral school working with a population of people who have most certainly been hammered by late-stage capitalism far worse than I have. Some of these kids were so poor their families couldn't afford to fix holes in the walls leading outdoors to the harsh Maine winter. When you realize kids are growing up in such environments in this very country, no amount of "hard work" within the "American Dream" is going to significantly lift this population, in most cases, out of poverty. I have seen what the rightward drift has done to individuals and families in the form of addiction, poverty, and the inevitable issues that plague these homes as a result, and I believe we should be educating the masses so something meaningful can be done about it. Personally, I started investigating the way the world works not only out of curiosity, but to make sense out of my own situation as a person living paycheck to paycheck, living at home, and working a thankless, brutal, yet highly-necessary, job with impoverished people as other members of society hoarded tens of billions of dollars in wealth – some of which contribute absolutely nothing meaningful to humanity, others who never worked a day in their life. I now teach to try to do my part in calling attention and hopefully eventually fixing some of these issues. If we don't reckon with these types of problems, I fear we will continue to see widespread unrest and a state that deals with it not by providing a floor for people to stand on, but with a boot to the face and a knee on the neck. When you add the issue of the impending climate disaster and the inevitable destabilization that will cause, this type of education is a necessity.

Drawing upon a plethora of wonderful books and sources I have consumed daily for many years, I have developed a curriculum that gets kids thinking about the world around them, about democracy, journalism, information, bias, politics, parties, issues, empathy, and much more. As I reach a time when I myself am starting a family, I firmly believe the world itself depends upon these lessons taking hold in public consciousness. The alternative to turning things around is to continue this incessant rightward drift by both major US political parties, and frankly this looks like an utterly horrifying place – income disparities climbing alongside the dawn of trillionaires, unlimited warrantless spying, endless and expensive warfare, a gutted public sector as wealth, power, and influence is consolidated in unelected and unaccountable hands, and of course, most importantly, the looming climate disaster. We can't sit around and wait for the powerful to have an Ebenezer Scrooge epiphany, we need to educate the masses.

I see no other entity that could possibly set the record straight as thoroughly and quickly besides a public institution. Not colleges, not podcasts, not even the internet. Teachers are a gift to this country, but we must come through to avert the rightward drift scenario as described above. Since we impact such a huge percentage of people, it seems we are poised for this incredibly important task.

The first part of the book will deal with the first semester of my curriculum where we cover the basics of journalism, the arguments for teaching bias in the classroom, and why bias in the classroom isn't necessarily a bad thing. The second half of the book will take a look at the second semester where we look at media literacy from fake news to corporate media to critical thinking to conspiracy theories to conspiracies.

I don't claim to have all of the answers. In fact one of the primary lessons I try to drive home in my classes is that the world is so complex and intricate it's difficult for anyone to have all of the answers, which is precisely why we shouldn't be satisfied with simplistic solutions or supposed answers to complicated problems. It's precisely why we should be open-minded and hear all sorts of points of view. But I do believe the curriculum I have created in my journalism class (and my other English classes where I feature similar lessons on power, labor, collective action, etc.) is a very solid baseline of topics and ideas for every single teenager in America to consider as they become civically minded and aware human beings while they make their way into the world looking out for their own self-interests. I also maintain that plenty of adults could benefit from taking my journalism class, but barring a *Billy Madison* situation, I don't see that happening. So I wrote this book. Whether you're a teacher looking for ideas, an adult who wants a better handle on how to sift through media, or a parent demanding more from their school system, I am glad my work has found its way into your hands.

Chapter 1

September – The Basics of Journalism and Objectivity

What does democracy mean to you?
What about a free press?
Why is a free press and access to accurate information so vital within a democracy?

I ask these questions of my high school journalism students on day one. Kids are intuitive and bright. Though they've possibly never invested much thought in these questions, the answers are there – but sometimes they need to be asked point blank to get the wheels turning. Though some answers sort of miss the point or produce misunderstandings, when presented with such questions a lot of the students loosely understand what the class is going to be about on the first day. They suspect democracy and a free press respectively give the people a voice and inform the masses, so are both therefore a moral good.

Do you watch/listen to/read the news? Or do you find it too depressing? Perhaps too complex?

The answers to this question are relatively consistent – "No, yes, and yes." Let's face it, many adults would answer these questions similarly. Between a 24-hour news cycle that changes rapidly and fixates on negative stories (while sadly omitting perhaps even more important issues that would inherently damn the political duopoly) and a social media that spreads content rapidly, it can be easy to drown in the tidal wave of misconception and disinformation. Some end up allowing the news to heavily influence their thinking, others may shut it off entirely out of frustration. Given our media landscape and the amount of people too disenfranchised to vote, I would say neither outcome has been stellar.

The first set of questions feature wonderful answers by thoughtful high school kids. The second set reveals that many students are too overwhelmed to tackle the task of making sense of the world due to the sheer volume and nature of the news. Information itself has been, probably inadvertently, used as a form of censorship. Flooding the airwaves and internet with bad and misleading takes, outright lies, and disinformation can often obscure truths. If the truth is not accepted or known, and within a supposed democracy we're supposed to act based on what we the people know, we're going to end up with increasingly absurd outcomes in our elections, our response to politics, and in turn our public policy that shapes the world around us. If people are going to be in charge, an educated populace is vital. Echoing the sentiments of Aristotle, Astra Taylor illustrates beautifully in her book *Democracy May Not Exist, but We'll Miss It When It's Gone* that democracy is the best system available. As we contemplate this reality, we must in turn understand that ruling elites who have so much power over the information supply (and political process, and wealth) have every reason in the world to make sure the populace is misled, confused, and tired as a means of meeting their own self-interests that benefit a select few instead of the masses.

As Taylor points out in her book,

Adopting a worldview rooted in seventeenth-century conceptions of the social contract, Americans tend to see government as a threatening entity from which citizens must be protected. So while most advanced democracies offer their citizens a range of public welfare options (single-payer healthcare, subsidized childcare, free higher education, arts and journalism funding, and so on), the United States has taken a very different path. In the name of freedom of choice, Americans must seek employment that provides insurance benefits as a perk, lest they join the ranks of millions who have gone bankrupt due to medical debt; hire nannies to watch their offspring while they work, or if they are too poor, leave the kids home alone; borrow tens of thousands of dollars for education that they hope will land them a job that will remunerate them enough to repay their student loans; and be exposed to a culture that is overwhelmingly funded by advertising revenue, which means the privileging of expression primarily designed to help marketers sell products.

Americans increasingly flirt with simply allowing corporate overlords to dictate what happens in this country. Jeff Bezos is on track to become the world's first trillionaire as he actually hit $200 billion in net worth in 2021 despite the effects of COVID-19. The Waltons inherited their fortune. Even our president was a millionaire by age 5 and inherited $5-10 million per year from his daddy into his 50s. All the while, monetary influence has captured our political process and information supply, and a great many people gleefully cheer this on as though the ultra-wealthy share the same interests as the common working person.

Government and press working for the people

The Taylor quote, of course, is not to say that governments should be blindly trusted – far from it. It is to point out what a public sector might be capable of with an educated and engaged populace exercising their power.

One doesn't have to look far to find governments run amok. North Korea, of course, is essentially straight out of *1984* (I also teach freshman English and *1984* is a phenomenal book to help illustrate the importance of information as a sort of introduction to my journalism class, where I do more with the weaponization of language, "Orwellian" language, if you will. It's also a great book to introduce class conflict). Our own government obviously has a dark history of its own: the false flags such as the Gulf of Tonkin, illegally performing experiments on human subjects in MK-Ultra, the Tuskegee Syphilis Experiment, COINTELPRO, torture and drone assassination programs, warrantless surveillance, the list goes on and on. Additionally, as the group Represent Us illustrates in their YouTube series, which makes great material for making this point, Congress "literally doesn't care what we think." Citing extensive Princeton studies, it becomes quite clear who Congress works for – the ruling elites and the almighty dollar, not the people.

But how do we know about these things while North Koreans are left either ignorant of the truth or completely helpless to do anything about the lies due to the oppressive regime? The answer is great journalists and access to information. The more we know in self-advocacy for our own interests than the better we will be as a society. We don't know what we don't know.

This is exactly why Donald Trump has been unrelenting in his criticism of the press. He lies constantly and incessantly fosters a culture in which only he holds the answers and everyone else is a liar who needn't be listened to. His word is real, everything else is "fake news."

What's a bit trickier to unearth is how Barack Obama was in many ways worse than Trump on this issue. As many journalists have reported through the years, including Michael Enright of CBC, "Obama's justice department tapped reporters' phones, dragged reporters into court, and prosecuted three times as many cases targeting leakers than all previous administrations combined."

He went on,

Take the case of James Risen, a good reporter for the New York Times. The Obama justice department spent *seven years* – *seven* – in court, trying to get Risen to reveal his sources... In another case, the Obama White House went after a Fox

News reporter who was trying to get information about North Korea's nuclear arsenal...In public court documents, Obama's attorneys actually called the reporter a conspirator against the United States...The administration dug up and scoured records of nearly 100 Associated Press reporters and editors...Throughout the *eight years* of the administration, the Obama White House singled out Fox News for special attention...Said one Obama communications aide: "We're going to treat them the way we treat an opponent...[Trump] may be guilty of many things, politically and privately...But in the case of freedom of the press, his bark has been far worse than his bite. For real threats to press freedom, you have to look back to Barack Obama and his administration.

Now, in the case of Fox News's evening lineup, their disinformation campaign is most certainly a problem to be dealt with – it's a problem I deal with later in this book, and an issue I tackle in class. But is a reporter working for Fox doing a story on North Korea's nuclear arsenal really something that should be silenced? And should a president have the power to silence it? The journalist and appreciation of democracy in me thinks not. An Obama fan that doesn't want to hear the truth about their boy to maintain that rosy picture is no different than a fanatical Trump supporter who shouts "fake news" at whatever they don't want to hear.

The press *should* be adversarial toward the powerful. It should exist to inform the masses. It should exist to educate the public. We delve into the issues with corporate media later in the class, but it's helpful to point out what real journalism *should* look like, even if it can be hard to come by when following the large corporate sources. Journalists should not be partisan cheerleaders; they should be telling the public what is going on. They should be reporting the details whether it's a Democrat or a Republican (or both!) doing something wrong, not reporting based on omission and emphasis in the name of preserving party-image. Furthermore, we should trust and support journalists who dare to challenge the powerful.

How news articles should be written

In class we cover a lot of heavy topics briefly early on and then move on to the basics of journalism.

I show them the nut graf and inverted pyramid along with multiple examples of how this generally works in local newspapers and the Associated Press. A lede sentence and nut paragraph is written to give us the basic gist of the story, followed by more in-depth, additional information in the middle paragraphs, and finally interesting information at the end that isn't necessarily extremely important to the initial story.

The reason is not only to give readers the main point of the story right in the first few sentences so they can get a broad sense of the goings on in their world or community quickly, but also due to the nature of print newspapers in general. You can pack a bunch of stories on the front page of a section with a basic sense of what happened without even diving into the rest of the paper or individual story (which is why we see "continued on A24" in print).

This is important to go over in a journalism class not only because it offers a (I would say welcomed) alternative to essay writing, but it also gets students working on syntax and basic writing skills in their written assignments (in short, lots of my writing lessons are about omitting unnecessary words and avoiding clunkiness). Additionally, print news media is sadly increasingly outdated and archaic (its demise is one of the reasons I am teaching in the first place) so going over newspapers serves as an interesting juxtaposition of future units on obtaining information from the internet.

The nature of print media offered a bit more time to take a second and digest what was happening in the world. Fewer sources of information readily available decades ago had pros and cons. On one hand we didn't have reactionary 24-hour news cycles constantly fighting for clicks and attention using the most inflammatory headlines or flimsy sources, but on the other hand there was likely a more agreed-upon reality. On one hand we didn't have an overload of disinformation, but on the other hand we have a lot more independent options now with access to more populist and left-leaning publications, stories, and narratives that would have gone ignored by the big corporate gatekeepers in decades-past.

We also discuss the rules of attribution and interviewing. Reporters must take solid notes, try their hardest to be objective, and dig into the story by asking interesting and thought-provoking questions of their subject.

After looking at several examples and resources, when students have a basic understanding of how news articles are written and interviews are conducted, I send them out on a couple of assignments.

The first assignment is an interview with a classmate. Their goal is to find something unique about their subject, find out what their classmate is all about, and focus on that as the main point of the piece. They have their subjects go on record (whatever they say on the record can be written in the piece), interview one another, and complete a short story about their partner. This not only gets the students talking to one another at the top of the year, but also is a decent introduction to the basics of interviewing and writing news articles.

Before the second assignment of the year, we look at a few more examples of news stories in the local newspaper and online. I show them articles from local reports and the Associated Press because these sources generally try to remain as objective as possible – this serves as a fantastic juxtaposition for opinion writing in the next part of the class, and sadly, for the corporate media unit as well.

We pay attention to how the sentences and phrases of these types of articles are extremely matter of fact, no room for the reporter's own opinion on the matter. They are doing their best simply to state what happened, and I explain to them that editors at publications that value this sort of journalistic approach will do the same thing. We get into issues with inherent bias, emphasis, and omission in the news, but that will be covered in a later chapter.

When I first began teaching this class, I thought how wonderful it would be to have kids cover stories in their communities, or even stories of the goings on in the school. While I wouldn't rule that out in the future, it's difficult because I only have them under my guidance during class time, and a lot of them don't have access to transportation and things like that to go out and cover stories. So I had to manufacture my own event for them to cover so the whole class could be on the same page.

My solution was to play an episode of *The Office* in which a specific event happens that could certainly be a newsworthy article. Sure, some kids hate the show (most seem to enjoy it), but they're generally just happy to get to watch TV in class.

An episode that worked for me is from season 5, episode 14, *Stress Relief*. The episode begins with a disgruntled Dwight Schrute, who had just given a training on fire prevention that apparently no one paid attention to, so he blocked all exits and started a contained fire inside of the office which set off smoke alarms and caused massive panic in the building. One of his co-workers, Stanley Hudson, actually ended up suffering a heart attack which caused corporate headquarters to have to deal with reprimanding Schrute and his boss, Michael Scott.

The episode works for multiple reasons. *The Office* is filmed as though it was a reality show capturing simply what employees at a paper company were up to on a daily basis, so it feels sort of "real." In the episode there are literally interviews with the characters essentially breaking the fourth wall and talking right into the camera (and I also do a press conference where I answer questions from my student journalists on behalf of the characters). Because it naturally fits into the inverted pyramid. The main event of the story happens in the first 5 minutes of the show, followed by the in-depth details and results of Schrute's actions thereafter. The episode ends with stuff that is most certainly not essential to the main story, which of course goes at the end of a news article. Ultimately, it ends up being a great test in discovering whether students can write these news articles and remain objective by simply telling readers what happened without any obvious bias or opinion on the matter getting in the way.

Understanding objectivity is a topic we return to in the second semester when we discuss media literacy, but it is introduced early in the class. Though bias is an extremely slippery subject to cover and difficult, if not impossible, to fully avoid (as discussed in the next chapter), it's worth at least attempting to guide students into thinking about objectivity versus subjectivity.

The students hear with their own ears the answers from students in their interviews. They see with their own eyes Dwight Schrute blocking off all exits and starting a small fire in a trash can. Though it's trickier for them to actually write their story free of any obvious opinions, it at least opens the door for discussion on objectivity versus opinion. As I read their stories I leave extensive notes not only on their punctuation, grammar, and syntax, but also on their ability to remain objective and just give the facts. Sure, you might think Dwight Schrute is a selfish lunatic psychopath for pulling this stunt, but you can't (or shouldn't) deliver that opinion in a news story.

I believe getting them to think about this concept is a great way to begin the class and to get them to start thinking about what sort of information they are receiving. When their parents have Fox News or MSNBC on at night, is Sean Hannity giving the facts free from his opinion when he suggests the election was "stolen"? Is Rachel Maddow just reporting what happened when it comes to Trump potentially being a Russian secret agent, or is she peddling a baseless conspiracy theory on live television? Or are both of these partisan hacks a couple of crybabies who love their party more than actually informing the public?

Consumers of the news in a properly functioning democracy should be able to tell the difference between someone's opinion and fact whether it's a random Facebook post or published on a credible news outlet. As the line becomes increasingly blurred, it's more important than ever. In the next part of class we begin the tricky task of analyzing bias in the news.

Chapter 2

October/November – Bias and Opinion

"Ellen DeGeners and George W. Bush's friendship is what makes America great," read an October 8 headline by Dave Guerin in *The Philadelphia Inquirer*.

"Dear Ellen: The Problem With George W. Bush Is Not His Beliefs – It's His War Crimes," read an October 8 headline by Mendhi Hasan in *The Intercept*.

Before the COVID-19 pandemic and unprecedented unrest in protest of racial oppression and police brutality, the friendship between Degeneres and Bush made headlines briefly. Though any two differing stories would work, this particular story is pretty tame and straightforward, so I used it to introduce bias to my students.

We looked at the *Inquirer* article first. After lamenting an unknown period of time where both parties were just best pals trying to make the world a better place Guerin concludes his piece with,

The country needs more of those moments and less of the Twitter bullying, both from the left and right...So, what's the solution? Stop tweeting and start talking. Take the time to listen and reflect on what the other person is saying and recognize that our differences are our greatest strengths. The ability to forge and retain friendships across party, racial, and ethnic lines is what makes our America a country worth cherishing.

Holy platitude, Batman! It would be great if the argument was, "don't be friends with people from the opposite party," but that wasn't the root of the disgust. Talking heads love party lines.

Consequently, consumers of these pundits also love party lines. It's the reason why, when you're in a debate with a Trump supporter about an issue like immigration and they say, "yeah well what about Obama? He deported a ton of people." A typical business-as-usual Democrat would fumble through some sort of bullshit answer "whatabouting" Trump or claiming it was different when Obama deported a record amount of people, but someone truly left on the spectrum (or just in-tune and objective) would say, "yeah deported lots of people and built the facilities." Though Trump did go a step further with child separation policy which was enacted, per his own admission, to deter immigrants, the Obama administration did deport 2 million people, and Trump supporters aren't mistaken for pointing that out. Meanwhile, perhaps these people wouldn't be trying to leave their homes at all if American imperialism hadn't destabilized Latin America in the dirty wars of the 80s.

But at any rate, the argument never was to not be friends with a Republican. The argument is that it's problematic that Ellen, an out-of-touch multi-millionaire, seems to ignore Bush's brutal history as a war criminal and speaks highly of him despite this reality.

In Hasan's article, he highlights the litany of people Bush policy effected directly, the body count on his hands, the torture, and the pure destruction he unleashed particularly in the Middle East.

To really make the point it is essential to show my students the *Inquirer* article first. If they, like any other person who knows the reality of Bush, read the Inquirer article second, they would immediately know the entire thing was a bad faith argument that in no way even remotely touches upon the actual grievances people were making. They read the *Inquirer* piece and essentially say, "yeah, that's true, we should be civil and be able to get past our political differences in day-to-day interactions."

But after reading the nuance in Hasan's article, their opinion on the matter changes. Maybe it isn't so admirable that Ellen is so out of touch when it comes to Bush's mark on recent history. Maybe it's not that cool to call a guy who committed war crimes a "kind, sweet man" when we consider how people in the Middle East must view him. None of this is to say that people with different beliefs shouldn't be friends, but it at least raises the question – is the Bush/Degeneres friendship really that simple? A visible multi-millionaire using her platform to rehabilitate a terrible president who was a war criminal? Should this really be celebrated?

Two articles like this illustrate a number of points. For one thing, you can find pretty much any take on anything online these days. There is no agreed-upon reality, particularly for issues with a lot of gray area and moral questions, but as we see with COVID-19, the 2020 election, or the climate crisis, even cold hard facts are somehow left in question in broader public discourse. The students begin to realize that you really need to cross reference, draw from various sources, and make sure whatever is initially read hasn't suffered the process of omission and emphasis to create the desired narrative – in this case making it seem like Bush isn't so bad after all, harkening back to days of "normalcy" when "normal" was getting involved in unnecessary wars, eroding civil liberties, and doing similar things Trump is doing now (I would argue Bush was far worse than Trump in terms of policy) but with a more polished facade.

Two articles such as these make a great introduction to bias. The same thing is discussed but two very different articles are written. Guerin's agenda is to preserve a favorable image of Bush and American parties, not to reckon with the actual arguments. Hasan points out the ugliness of American imperialism. It allows for some fine discussions on what can be drawn from the articles. The students take away some great stuff from each piece: we should be able to talk with people with different views – but even so, perhaps befriending former presidents when you're a public figure like Ellen is a bit more complicated. They're also often blown away at how altered a legacy such as Bush's can become after uncomfortable truths are cleansed by corporate media, celebrities, and parties themselves.

These articles are a nice starting point to get into bias, which is an increasingly difficult concept to cover. Does bias matter? Does everyone have a bias? Does bias affect what a reporter or columnist writes? Is it possible to avoid or to quantify bias?

Of course, many have tried, but it can be a tricky business. Take, for example, the famous Ad Fontes Media Bias Chart created by lawyer Vanessa Otero (many have probably seen it, if not check it out online).

The chart's methodology has changed throughout the years. According to their website regarding the current chart: "During this project, nearly 1800 individual articles and TV news shows were rated by at least three analysts with different political views (left, right and center). We had 20 analysts, each analyst having analyzed about 370 articles and about 17 TV shows. Each analyst rated approximately three articles from each of the over 100 news sources available for viewing on the Chart. As a result, we have nearly 7,000 individual ratings."

That sounds like a good faith effort at first glance, but who are these individuals? Who determined what the spectrum of "left, right and center" looked like? In some countries such as Norway, a politician like Bernie Sanders, inaccurately viewed as a communist in America, is thought of as *slightly right-of-center.* In America, a bank-coddling corporatist like Barack Obama was painted as a communist by the GOP and right-wing media while a right-wing corporatist like Mitt Romney is supposedly a "centrist." Even in 2020 the Trump campaign somehow got away with painting the corporatist right winger Joe Biden as a "socialist" or "communist," which is well-beyond anything resembling honesty, reality, or a command of the political spectrum – but who could expect anything else from a man that simultaneously attacked Biden for being "weak on crime," *and* said he "lost the left" for proudly authoring the "tough on crime" bill.

Who is making these determinations about left, right, and center? When you look at how the chart is analyzed, MSNBC is just as far left as *Jacobin*. *Jacobin* is an independent leftist publication; MSNBC is a gigantic corporation whose highest paid contributor (Rachel Maddow – more on her later) makes $7 million a year. MSNBC's coverage was regarded as highly favorable to Biden while it slammed Bernie Sanders, meanwhile *Jacobin* openly celebrates the philosophy of Karl Marx, who is undeniably much further left than anything Sanders ever proposed. The point most certainly is not to say my political spectrum is more accurate; I think the whole thing is too subjective to make such a determination, but any bias chart that puts corporate MSNBC and anti-privatization *Jacobin* in the same spectrum is quite problematic. Placing those two sources on the same economic or political spectrum completely obfuscates truly left politics.

Dave Van Zandt of mediabiasfactcheck.com has a similar process in which he rates different websites for bias. Again, what is Van Zandt and his team's bias?

None of this is meant to be nihilistic. The last thing I want is for kids to throw up their hands and say, "everything is biased, I guess I am done here." In fact, I even have them use the Media Bias Chart for different assignments, but I simply make sure they realize that the chart itself carries a sort of hidden bias which should not be ignored, the chart should not be seen as an arbiter of truth, and its contents should most certainly not be seen as a foregone conclusion on par with objective facts. Being able to cross reference is potentially the main lesson here. If you hear a great take, or hold a certain belief, dare to be open to other takes and information that might upend your existing beliefs and opinions. Hold on to those opinions, but with an open mind, if an argument comes along rooted in fact and evidence that fatally challenges your beliefs, don't be afraid to evolve as a thinker. Personally, I went from being an Obama fanboy to viewing him as a corporate Wall Street toady, and I think I am better for it. When people challenged my thinking, I got tired of defending someone who wasn't acting in my interests and therefore didn't deserve my defense.

We go further in depth regarding bias from sources and their process of omission and emphasis in later units. This unit provides a wonderful time early in the year for students to begin to consider what it is they believe in. I also take the time to help them learn their own bias.

There are multiple tests and quizzes out there that will help make sense of a person's bias. PoliticalCompass.org provides a chart which plots a test-taker both on an economic spectrum and on an authoritarian or libertarian spectrum. 8Values is another solid one that gets more into ideology. AllSides.com and ISideWith.com are centered around US politics (and therefore, in my view, less-favorable than the two mentioned previously) and give test-takers the best option of who to vote for – to their credit they do include third party candidates. Though the results should be taken with a grain of salt, these tests ask pretty in-depth questions and offer different tiers of answers.

Then, of course, there's *Turning Point UK*'s version of a political bias test. It asks a mere ten yes or no questions such as "Is aspiration a good thing?" Answering "no" means you're a leftist commie scum bag, answering "yes" means you're a good conservative and should therefore consume *Turning Point*. Of course, like so much on the Right, this is but a caricature of the other tests, a self-serving mechanism that clearly has an agenda, but it does clearly illustrate that even these tests do indeed carry a bias with them because human beings made them, and human beings have a hard time not being biased. In the case of Charlie Kirk's *Turning Point USA* the entire point is either to peddle right-wing brain-rot and muddy the waters so people remain confused about what they actually believe, which of course is fertile grounds for disinformation, or to haplessly attempt to convince people they're definitely right wing because they view "aspiration" as a "good thing." Either way, it's insufferable, which of course is merely my opinion.

The tests can not only be a lot of fun for the kids, but also reveal a lot. I believe this is particularly beneficial when students are actively thinking about the flaws with the tests, so they take in the results in a level-headed, thoughtful manner.

Around this time I am looking for students to pick up on something very important. A main theme of all of this is to get students to understand that bias and agendas are something to keep in mind *every time* they consume information.

OK, Mr Shain...so what's your bias?

It's music to my ears, and it happens in every single journalism block by one of the thoughtful, usually more outspoken, students.

So what's my play here? A lot of people would say, "You can't possibly reveal your bias to these high school kids. What are you thinking?"

Really? Whether you're Republican or Democrat, given the points I have already tried to make in the weeks leading up to this moment, you want the teacher who has admittedly and outspokenly adamantly opposed both of our corporate-coddling parties to present himself as an infallible arbiter of truth? Fine with me, I guess, but it doesn't seem right. So should I not instead admit my bias to these students who are completely justified and wise to ask for the bias of the person who is dispensing information?

No, this doesn't mean the class becomes a "you should think exactly the way I do" class. However, when a question comes up, such as, "what's your bias, Mr Shain?" I think the students have a right to know answers to certain things; lying to them by claiming I am an arbiter of truth and therefore have no bias is clearly a dangerous game. I am extremely proud to say that a slew of right-leaning students have made a point of saying how fairly they thought I ran the class. I would never let a student's political belief affect their grade, and if they thought I did I would be very open to hearing their case about the possibility that my bias was getting in the way, but I am yet to run into any sort of problem like that. The point of my class is to try to offer insights on *how* to think, not *what* to think.

Furthermore, any sort of bias impressed upon a high school kid is going to come from their home. You hear the right-wing claim all of the time that schools are indoctrinating kids, but I am not certain there is much proof of that, it seems parents do a great job of that on their own. And of course, anyone who opened up the book randomly to this section asking, "well why teach politics at all?" should go back to the introduction to hear the arguments I made to this point previously.

When I speak subjectively in class, such as, "I don't think healthcare could or should be so expensive in this country," I accompany such opinions with a "Mr Shain opinion alert," which the kids get a kick out of and also appreciate. Though they don't get the same luxury of honesty from the sources themselves with the claims they run into online, I think they deserve the alert from their teacher. I think they also deserve to know when they go into a history class that depending if a teacher is using the account of American history through the eyes of Howard Zinn, who wrote the left-leaning *A People's History of the United States*, or from Larry Schwiekart, who wrote the American/economy-centric *A Patriot's History of the United States*, the class is going to look quite a bit different. I believe this is an important lesson on the quest to becoming a savvy media consumer, but I am still not an all-knowing, all-powerful arbiter of truth. I may be emphasizing something I shouldn't be emphasizing or omitting something I should have said – I may have a great class here, but I'm only human.

Writing a column

Now it's time for students to start thinking about their own beliefs and writing their own columns about an issue of their choice.

Though we understand the Media Bias Chart carries its own bias, we can use it as a loose guideline. In researching their topic, I have them look to accessible news websites to find facts and evidence to support their opinion. Cross-referencing and replying to counterarguments will make for the best columns.

Since the first columns we looked at regarding the Degeneres/ Bush friendship were a bit superficial, I choose a bit more of a substantive topic just before the assignment: homelessness.

We look at several pieces of content on homelessness – an article from the Democratic Party's media arm, MSNBC, the Republican Party's arm, Fox News, opinion pieces by *Jacobin*, Jon Stewart's *The Daily Show*, a PragerU video, a Stephen Crowder column, and finally a news article by the Associated Press.

We don't have time to endlessly peruse around each source, so I choose articles that I personally believe will illustrate typical coverage by each source on a topic like homelessness, articles that have made the rounds on social media until they were bumped out by the next wave of the 24-hour news cycle. I want to reiterate that any content a teacher chooses to present to class is filtered through a process of emphasis and omission which reveals their own bias. The articles I decided to present are my own bias shining through. My students at this point are savvy enough to know that instead of naively believing that I am an arbiter of truth just because I am their teacher, just as they will be savvy enough to know to cross reference information from politicians, news anchors, pundits, or future teachers. I chose to use homelessness as the vehicle for making a point in my English class. This is because I know a bit about income inequality and care deeply that there are people who live out on the streets in the richest country in the world.

The MSNBC headline blares, "Trump says homelessness hurting real estate prestige, will destroy cities." The Fox News headline shouts, "Former San Francisco mayoral candidate: Years of liberal policies have caused homelessness 'tragedy.'"

The two articles are painfully short, hyper-partisan, finger-point at the opposite party, and ultimately don't say too much of anything. This is foreshadowing our unit on corporate media in the second semester. The crux of the problem, according to these sources and the articles that take 60 seconds to read, is clearly the fault of the other party. Further analysis on economic structures, government programs, and other complex issues are mentioned only briefly within the articles. The main point of each article, however, is to make the other side look bad and blame the other party, not the brand of capitalism that dominates both party ideologies, for the awful reality of homelessness.

We then look at the 2017 *Associated Press* article which is more of a deep dive into the homeless problem in San Francisco and Seattle. We observe a few differences between the MSNBC/ Fox reporting and the *AP* reporting immediately. For one thing it takes longer than 60 seconds to read. It features pictures of homeless camps. It features a bunch of interviews with actual homeless people. It goes much further in depth than the MSNBC/ Fox "reporting" and serves to tell a story as to what is going on in the world of homelessness rather than try to lay blame for the problem itself vaguely on the other party.

"I've got economically zero unemployment in my city, and I've got thousands of homeless people that actually are working and just can't afford housing," said Seattle City Councilman Mike O'Brien in the *AP* article. "There's nowhere for these folks to move to. Every time we open up a new place, it fills up."

The article continues,

Homelessness is not new on the West Coast. But interviews with local officials and those who serve the homeless in California, Oregon and Washington – coupled with an Associated Press review of preliminary homeless data – confirm it's getting worse. People who were once able to get by, even if they suffered a setback, are now pushed to the streets because housing has become so expensive.

All it takes is a prolonged illness, a lost job, a broken limb, a family crisis. What was once a blip in fortunes now seems a life sentence.

"Most homeless people I know aren't homeless because they're addicts," said Tammy Stephen, 54, who lives at a homeless encampment in Seattle. "Most people are homeless because they can't afford a place to live."

When we couple this with Seattle's and San Francisco's booming economies and lavish areas despite their homeless problem, it really gets the wheels turning. The interviews with the working-homeless in particular should be quite eye-opening to anyone reading about this travesty, especially teenagers who are at no shortage of empathy generally speaking.

So what do different political solutions have to say about this problem? Here is where we turn to our conversation on bias and opinion writing after a short stint looking at the *AP* piece – which we also discuss could be argued to carry an inherent bias because the reporters are only human, they are deciding on what details to omit or emphasize from the story they're putting together.

Here's conservative darling Stephen Crowder offering up his solutions in his own publication, *Louder with Crowder*:

I'd advise the people of Seattle do the same since the two cities have too much in common. When it comes to the homeless, maybe don't subsidize their illegal activities. Like providing clean "injection sites." Think of it this way. If you don't want to attract more of something, you don't set up a breeding ground for it. If I could use an analogy for a smidgen of your time. Say you're dealing with wasps. It's summertime, so hear me out. If you want to have fewer wasps in your yard, would you designate an area of your yard where the wasps could come and get clean sugar water? Or would you make your yard as uninviting as you could for the wasps? No, setting traps isn't the same. That's trying to eliminate wasps by catching them. That's not what San Francisco is doing. San Francisco is just making it easier for the wasps to sting, sending the people scurrying.

After reading the *AP* article first, the kids understand that Crowder not only insinuates the homeless are all addicted to drugs (and even if this were true, why vilify them for it? Might there be a reason for it?) but also compares "the homeless," such as working-homeless people in Seattle, to a pest that needs extermination or removal.

He goes on,

I have another idea, which may be naive. What would happen if the city stopped funneling money into the homeless problem entirely, and let private charities work their magic? Kind of seems like after all the hundreds of millions the government has thrown at it, nothing is sticking. What if more city funds were channeled into law enforcement, and law enforcement were allowed to enforce laws? I know right. Let's not get crazy.

Another idea: more of San Francisco's upper crust elites should be putting more political pressure on San Francisco's bureaucrats to actually solve the problem, instead of leveraging the problem as an election platform. Goes to taxation without representation. If the city officials aren't solving the city's problems, then the city's wealthy taxpayers need to flex their economic muscles.

Here Crowder recommends that the same private sector that pays little or avoids taxes and is hiking rents in these areas should "work their magic" and be charitable. He also, unbelievably, dumps on government spending to help the homeless, but also suggests law enforcement, which though not "socialism," is often indeed paid for by tax dollars, might be the answer. Of course, since it's Stephen Crowder, he doesn't take a moment to analyze how much it might cost to start doing law enforcement to people like Tammy Stephen because he views the homeless as actual parasites rather than human beings who might be homeless for a variety of different reasons. He also goes into no detail as to how the private sector would decide to do things differently than government programs, or why we should wait around for these entities to be charitable rather than tax them accordingly. He also never considers that if throwing money at the situation doesn't work, we could put the means of production into the hands of the people instead of naively relying on a handful of unelected, unaccountable capitalists to solve serious issues like poverty and homelessness.

I truly don't believe it's hyperbole to say this is the general right-wing strategy on this and other issues. Law and order, personal responsibility, no government spending, and the naive reliance that perhaps charitable contributions will fix a problem like this even though there is very little evidence suggesting that might be true. Crowder is rather brash with his irrationally confident delivery, but he really does put all of the right-wing talking points out there in his article.

The kids aren't dumb. After being exposed to the *AP* article, they're not fooled by Crowder's in-your-face simplicity on this matter. I don't even need to share my own two cents in the classroom regarding the loudmouth Crowder, they are savvy enough at this point to pick apart his bullshit column on their own. If you aren't exposed to anything other than brain geniuses like Crowder, however, his story might sound appealing and make a lot of sense. Let's commit to making that possibility extremely unlikely.

In addition to the Crowder column, I play them a short interview with Dennis Prager on Fox News where he briefly whines about the homeless in a similar manner as Crowder, only to move quickly to promoting his new movie. This and a video of homeless camps with a caption that said, "what happens when the Left runs your city." It's all I could find on homelessness by Prager U. Try harder, Dennis.

The whole "California is run by Democrats so this is what leftist politics do to homelessness" routine is a great opportunity to illustrate that although California is indeed run by Democrats, the policies are not leftist or socialist by any means. While California is the fifth largest economy in the world, it still has a hell of a problem with homelessness. This is a rich state where its wealthiest are doing quite well, but the poorest continue to suffer. This reality lays waste to the idea of right-wing trickle-down economics: while the state has a booming economy on paper, it still features an obscene amount of people living below the poverty line. If trickle-down economics works, if capitalism is so great, why the issues in California? As Martin Luther King Jr. said, "This country has socialism for the rich, and rugged individualism for the poor."

So we take a look at another approach in dealing with homelessness that could actually be considered left wing. After reading a Jacobin article, *The Solution Is Social Housing*, which goes into detail explaining how to pay for millions of housing units, we look at a clip from Comedy Central, of all places. *The Daily Show*'s Hasan Minhaj did a 2015 segment on Salt Lake City, Utah's plan to combat homelessness called "The Homeless Homed." The concept is simple: give the homeless housing.

Director of the project Lloyd Pendleton explains in the segment that it has reduced homelessness by 72 percent and is actually less expensive than emergency runs and arrests ("law and order"). The segment interviews a recipient of the program, Russel Flowers, who humanizes the situation just as Tammy Stephens did in the *AP* article. Absent of course from right-wing narratives regarding this issue is any form of humanization – the exact opposite, in fact. Within *The Daily Show* segment, which notably does something people like Stephen Crowder refuse to do by acknowledging the legitimate position of the other side, are Fox News clips saying things like "we can't afford it" or claiming that poor people are living the high life because they have a refrigerator.

We look at the rebuttals to the Utah program. Most criticism discusses how the program hasn't completely eradicated homelessness, and how it does cost money and we have to keep throwing money at the program – but arresting them or policing them also costs money. Society costs money, civilization costs money. Should we treat these folks as humans or as wasps as Crowder so callously suggests?

A point to be made which is in no way hyperbolic is that I am actually in a closer financial position to a homeless person than I am an extremely wealthy person. I don't say this to the class, but their parents more-than-likely are as well. If I wasn't so lucky as to have a great family, friends, and in-laws to take me in if I lost my job, had a bad medical episode, or couldn't make ends meet, I could lose my house and end up on the street. This scenario, though unlikely thanks to my friends and family, is far more likely than me becoming a millionaire, let alone a billionaire, as a teacher at a public school. As Flowers says in his interview with Minhaj, why would anyone want to be poor or homeless? Contrary to the right-wing descriptions of the mooching homeless, it's not exactly living the dream to sleep on concrete or live in squalor.

Assignment time

Now they've got to put it all together. We've looked at a bunch of columns in class from a variety of political perspectives, we've seen different approaches to writing and presenting information, we've analyzed bias, now it's time to write their own columns.

I keep it very open-ended and let them write their opinion pieces on any issue that means a lot to them. I have received everything from columns on police brutality to arguing Kaepernick should stand for the anthem to a bunch on LGBTQ rights to homelessness after the lessons in class inspired them.

Before they begin, we take a look at George Lakoff's book *Don't Think Of An Elephant!* When he teaches the study of framing in his Cognitive Science 101 class in Berkeley, his first order of business is the following exercise:

> When I teach the study of framing, the first thing I do is I give my students an exercise. The exercise is: Don't think of an elephant! Whatever you do, do not think of an elephant. I've never found a student who is able to do this. Every word, like elephant, evokes a frame, which can be an image or other kinds of knowledge: Elephants are large, have floppy ears and a trunk, are associated with circuses, and so on. The word is defined relative to that frame. When we negate a frame, we evoke the frame.

I do the same with my class. Aside from a few wise guys who claim they have the ability to be completely clear-minded, most admit they thought of an elephant, or something closely related to an elephant even though I told them not to.

Lakoff introduces framing in the same book,

> Frames are mental structures that shape the way we see the world. As a result, they shape the goals we seek, the plans

we make, the way we act, and what counts as a good or bad outcome of our actions. In politics our frames shape our social policies and the institutions we form to carry out policies. To change our frames is to change all of this. Reframing is social change.

You can't see or hear frames. They are part of what cognitive scientists call the "cognitive unconscious" – structures in our brains that we cannot consciously access, but know by their consequences: the way we reason and what counts as common sense. We also know frames through language. All words are defined relative to conceptual frames. When you hear a word, its frame (or collection of frames) is activated in your brain.

Reframing is changing the way the public sees the world. It is changing what counts as common sense. Because language activates frames, new language is required for new frames. Thinking differently requires speaking differently.

Of course, a lot of this is pretty elevated stuff for high school kids and may be lost on some in their own work (which doesn't necessarily mean they won't be able to identify framing in other content), but I think it is worth noting as they begin writing their own columns. To me it illustrates that they need to go on the offensive with their language. They need to say what they mean, what they believe in, and adopt their own framing when making their point. If they argue for a similar approach to homelessness as Salt Lake City, for example, they should actively disregard the Crowder framing that the homeless are wasps that need to be exterminated, losers who asked for their situation, and criminals who should be arrested. They should work on telling their own version of the story, and in doing so set the record straight, write something fresh, and say what they mean rather than be tied down with the inhumane framing of the right wing. We see constantly the Democratic Party unable to escape the framing of the right wing – they join them in getting tough on crime, refuse to ban fracking, and refuse to acknowledge the obvious flaws of capitalism itself because they're tied to their wealthy donors. In the case of the Crowder article, why on earth would you adopt his framework? I encourage my students to do their research, view different sides and perspectives, and be tough in their convictions. Arguing to provide homes for wasps won't get one very far in advocating for homelessness, but arguing to house human beings (who may have fallen upon hard times for a variety of different reasons) for a cheaper cost than ER runs and law and order is obviously a much stronger framing of the issue.

I encourage students to pick controversial topics so they can actively respond to the arguments of the other side within their papers. If the topic is something everybody agrees upon, there isn't any room to acknowledge the other side and refute it. I find it helpful to have a class where we spend 15 minutes or so on a variety of topics, engaged in class discussion, hearing different opinions, being respectful, civil, and open-minded. This can help any students struggling to come up with a topic they are excited about, and the kids enjoy having their voices heard. For this I essentially just facilitate the discussion and make sure if it gets heated that everyone remains respectful. We've had moments where tensions grow high, but if done responsibly I think it's a great exercise in debating, being respectful, civil, and open to hearing opposing viewpoints.

Finally, it's time to begin writing. I want to give a quick note on my philosophy regarding assignments/homework: I give a ton of time in class to work on them, and I only give about 3-4 major assignments per semester with very little, if any, graded busywork – the closest thing I have to that is a class participation grade. Students essentially have to complete every assignment to some degree, because there are so few, and show up to class to get a decent grade. I give plenty of time in class because a lot of kids have a ton of stuff going on: working jobs, taking care of younger siblings while their parents work, sports, extra-extra-curricular activities, and just a basic social life are all things that teenagers have going on, not to mention all of their other classes piling on homework. The in-class work time gives me a chance to check in and help them if they need it, time for them to get their work done, and no excuses for not actually doing the assignment. I understand there are other philosophies on this, but this is mine in a nutshell.

I make sure the students are using at least three sources for their opinion pieces and cite their sources if they reference them in their column ("According to an *AP* report..."). I emphasize that they shouldn't just be giving their preconceived opinion on a topic and writing about it, they should think of a topic and then use all of the tools they've learned thus far in cross-referencing, researching, and then build their opinion based on facts and evidence.

When students complete their columns, I set aside another class for open debate and discussion on the variety of topics they have written about in their columns. Again, I play moderator here, which is even more necessary now as the students are more knowledgeable and engaged on their topics for this class discussion than they were before the assignment.

It's a lot of fun to see the kids become enthusiastic and engaged with the issues of the day. I think the best problem to have for this portion is getting them to calm down a little bit, reminding them that for the discussion to work only one person can be talking at once. When I have five hands go up with kids wanting to get their two cents in, whether I brought that out of them or simply provided the space for them to be engaged and passionate about an issue, I feel I have done my job.

The idea that none of that discussion should occur because "politics don't belong in the classroom" is far too dismissive of such important issues. To be frank, kids enjoy my class. They say things like, "it's nice to be learning about something important." They're teenagers. They're a few short years away from working, voting, potentially becoming politically active, etc. – some are already involved in these activities. They see adults get into this stuff and recognize it is important. They feel like they're engaged in something meaningful because they are. In English, we are afforded the opportunity to pick from a sea of material that will ultimately derive written and speaking assignments, which is incredibly important, but I have decided to double the impact by picking incredibly substantial and rich material to not only get kids better at writing and public speaking but also to become more civically minded and help them make sense of the way the world works. This most certainly is something to celebrate, not condemn, and I defy anyone who says otherwise.

Chapter 3

December – Bringing It All Together, Winding Down Semester 1

The first semester is a crash course in what the news can and should look like. We take a brief look at how articles should be written as unbiased as possible, the basics with the inverted pyramid, etc. We take a short preview of next semester when we see how corporate media sources enjoy simplistic and partisan messaging, and how the news can often omit and emphasize different narratives to perpetuate an agenda. We see in articles like the *Associated Press* story on homelessness on the West Coast that stories are often far more complicated than meet the eye. We see in examples of decent journalism that biases try to be put on the back burner in the name of telling a more objective story, and that a topic like homelessness is quite complicated and vast – solutions, whether from Crowder's *Louder with Crowder* or Stewart's *Daily Show*, are complex, not simple.

I would argue it's important for kids to be thinking about all of this stuff. Perhaps I was closed-minded and naive as a youngster and most other kids were able to figure this out on their own, but I recall viewing my teachers as arbiters of truth. Though I think teachers do their best, it's worth keeping in the back of your mind due to a variety of factors when consuming any information that there is likely more to the story, it's not as simple as things first appear. This lesson alone is important as the journalism class sets itself up for the second semester, which focuses on media literacy.

But first we have to wrap things up in the opening semester. One final assignment to tie in interviewing, the inverted pyramid, telling the facts, and even incorporating their opinion columns to a degree.

For the last assignment of the semester, the goal is to have conversations with peers and other people the students know and get them to "spill the tea" (though I like it and use it as the name of the assignment, their term, not mine) about the issue they just researched for their opinion column.

Their instructions are essentially to gage how their peers at school think about the issue they just researched for their opinion pieces. As they write it, the expectation is to keep in mind the inverted pyramid, to switch back to being unbiased reporters, and to be good interviewers that listen to what their subjects are saying and record it accurately. Since they have some knowledge on the topic, they will be able to ask good questions and also correct any misconceptions their subject may have in the interview – this, frankly, is a good trait to look for in a journalist. If they know their subject matter and their history, chances are they will ask better questions, adopt better framing, and ultimately deliver stories of a much more substantial nature.

I try to give them five steps for the assignment: 1. Prepare for the interview, as they in many ways already have by becoming acquainted with the topic they'll be asking their subjects about. 2. Craft questions about the topic at hand. 3. Listen intently to the answers provided by their subjects. 4. Record what they say accurately and in good faith. 5. Reread notes and consider any follow-up questions to ask the subjects to improve the story.

Since they have already hopefully completed the column, which is effective because they're also aware of their bias and what they might be emphasizing or omitting aspects of in their questions, they are already on the second part, which is crafting questions. I give them time in class to try to come up with at least ten questions to ask other students about their topic, or as many as they can with good ideas for follow-up questions ready to go.

When the class has their questions ready, I utilize the study halls (with the okay from the study hall monitor, of course) during my journalism blocks to make sure my students have plenty of subjects to interview during class hours. This serves multiple functions: it gets my students talking to other kids who may not agree with them about a sensitive topic. It gets kids who aren't even in the class thinking about a variety of topics. It gets people talking in person about material that too often seems too distant to think about, let alone do anything about, especially for high school kids.

During this time I go around and make sure students are on task or make myself available for an interview. The idea even beyond their final papers is to get people thinking and discussing the issues respectfully and civilly. It opens the door to ideas, discussion, and conversation. This alone is a way to move our country leftward again. Building relationships, realizing our interconnectedness, not seeing ourselves as just a bunch of individuals crawling our way through life is a valuable lesson, an important thing to consider that actively goes against the right-wing individualism lurking around on the internet.

The interviews and notes are worth points for the final project on their own, but when they put them together the plan is to write it like a news story from back in *The Office* assignment. Since this is a lot of new stuff for students between all of the topics we discuss, a new way of writing, interviewing, note taking, etc. I try to be understanding when I read how they actually get the results of their interviews on paper.

And with the completion of this assignment, the first semester is over.

* * *

When I first started teaching this class, my initial thought was to use it to start a school newspaper. In many ways that would be a lot of fun, sort of like a weekly or monthly yearbook featuring stories and content by students, but I believe that would sorely lack the type of substance that we end up encountering in the class I wound up with. My journalism class when I was in high school was, in many ways, great – it set me up nicely to be a reporter for a sort of feel-good community paper. I worked on my writing, I did some photojournalism, I learned the basics of the inverted pyramid, and other foundations of reporting.

But I don't think many other kids in that class spent any time working as a journalist in a small-time, or bigger, newspaper. We all, however, became adults who were expected to participate in a democracy and in doing so effectively have to consume news, understand the world, their country, their state, their community, and hopefully act on their best interests when they go to work, vote, organize, and participate in society. I had a lot of wonderful teachers, but I don't remember quite enough when it came to learning how to be a more aware, thoughtful, and engaged citizen when consuming information. I think teaching the basics of journalism and how it inherently relates to a functioning democracy is a wonderful step for anyone, but especially high school kids.

Once we observe how the news should look, and how it often looks if wielded by nefarious corporate sources or other entities with bad intentions or agendas, and how it impacts the consciousness of a country, we can move on to the finer points of these lessons – the media literacy portion of the class.

Part Two

Media Literacy

As long as the general population is passive, apathetic, diverted to consumerism or hatred of the vulnerable, then the powerful can do as they please, and those who survive will be left to contemplate the outcome.
Noam Chomsky

In 2020 COVID-19 gripped cities across the country – hundreds of thousands of Americans died from the virus along with millions of confirmed cases throughout the world. Yet prominent people in my community still shared baseless YouTube videos claiming the virus wasn't real, the reporting was fake, the numbers were inflated, the virus would magically "disappear after the election," coverage of the virus is an attempt to vaccinate people to death and institute marshal law, and other absurd declarations that were not backed by reality in any capacity.

In Maine, my home state, people were demanding to "open up" as early as mid-April 2020, only a month after the initial quarantine period. There were demonstrations in Augusta at the state capitol building. Armed with signs saying things like, "I want a haircut" or "I want to go out to eat," I even saw one crowd take a limousine to the rally as they took a group photo. Such demonstrations continued and expanded after Donald Trump lost the 2020 election, creating a hybrid rally of delusion featuring both "stop the steal" and anti-mask protestors – even as the virus surged, and zero evidence was brought forth to prove anything even resembling "election fraud."

There are multiple conversations to be had here. Giving people other ideas for how to deal with something like COVID is important to note. I personally thought these people had every reason to want to get back out and make money – after all, if the government is going to shut down livelihoods it needs to be prepared to take care of people economically – and get back to something they perceived to be "normal," but were ultimately completely misguided. Had they been demanding rent freezes, Universal Basic Income, and bailing out actual small businesses until this thing was under control, I'd have likely joined them. But the Left's solutions, which indisputably from a health standpoint would have done better dealing with the virus (even what little government intervention we did use still made the private sector's efforts pale in comparison), are not what they wanted. They demanded we "open up" and get back to work. The only way this messaging works is to either perform mental gymnastics or just outright say the cost of life isn't important.

But that's not the point I want to delve into in this book. The question is how and why the hell do I see on my social media elected officials, prominent local business owners, educators, salesmen, and a number of different types of functioning and successful adults sharing outright absurd disinformation such as the *Plandemic* video or other conspiracy theories surrounding COVID-19, George Floyd (videos claiming the whole thing was a staged event), Wayfair (claiming the company sells children inside of bureaus), or believing the baseless claims that Trump actually won the 2020 election?

For one thing, I do cut them some slack. As I wrote in a *Medium* article in May of 2020,

> Though it's tempting to write off our peers in the "open up" crowd (politicians and the wealthy excluded in this context) as sycophant bootlickers, I would argue it isn't entirely their fault. Our media has cried wolf many times before, whether it's Ebola, RussiaGate, Benghazi, Hillary's emails, the consent manufactured for the Iraq War, or any number of misleading or over-hyped stories peddled by far-right Fox News or moderate right CNN or MSNBC alike. Fox pretends it's newsworthy when Joy Villa wears a MAGA dress to the GRAMMYs. MSNBC and CNN pretend it's newsworthy when Alec Baldwin owns Donald Trump on SNL. If you point out that neither of these stories are newsworthy at all, people on either side get defensive for their tribe, even if they'd be able to identify their counterpart's story was empty horse shit.
>
> With such a low bar set for what is newsworthy within our big dumb 24-hour news cycle, as narratives grow increasingly partisan serving not to inform but to cheerlead

for either party, it's no surprise that we can't agree that COVID-19 is not a political issue but something we need to work together to stop. Though COVID-19 is a massive, worldwide pandemic, it's written off by skeptical Americans as just another hyper-partisan story. Though there are many great sources and journalists out there speaking truth to power, holding the powerful accountable, and doing so on behalf of working people (The Intercept, Matt Taibbi, Current Affairs, Jacobin, Democracy Now, The Nation to name a few) the media, constantly chasing profit, is the boy who cried wolf, and desperate people are increasingly open to insane stories about Dr Fauci being a mass murderer or Bill Gates (for some reason) wanting to put microchips in our arms. It seems they believe the conspiracy theories not necessarily because they're believable but rather simply because it's the opposite of what the distrusted mainstream narrative has to say. Though displaced and confused in this particular instance, their suspicion of corporate media makes sense, and it's corporate media's own fault.

Corporate media, social media, and cable news does us no favors in combating the tsunami of disinformation we see on a daily basis. Our 24-hour news cycle suffers attentional deficit disorder, the reporting is shallow and mundane, and the consent manufactured by corporate media when it comes to the Iraq War, RussiaGate, or making sure Hillary Clinton or Joe Biden is the Democratic Nominee turns out to be proven bullshit and it, I would say reasonably, makes people wary of their coverage. This gives people like Donald Trump a lane to point the finger at all of the wrong people and entities and fill the void with simplistic solutions and proposals with a bent toward privatization and law and order amid an already-privatized, already-militarized and incarcerated country. When a populace doesn't know any better, and journalism isn't doing its job, demagogues can help themselves to power and influence by giving simplistic, nationalistic, and xenophobic solutions to incredibly complex problems.

Frankly, I am here to argue our schools could be doing a hell of a lot better as well. There are often no Common Core Standards for the stuff I teach this semester. There is, to my knowledge, no built-in emphasis or infrastructure on teaching media literacy – and look at what type of adults this creates. Functioning adults who went through the American education system think it's somehow plausible that Anthony Fauci and Bill Gates have teamed up to vaccinate everyone to death because one video came out by some guy on YouTube who interviewed a quack of a doctor in the internet blockbuster *Plandemic*.

A state representative in the neighboring town actually defended her *Plandemic* advocacy by going on a long rant about how wonderful it is in America that we can all have opinions and disagree about stuff. Sure, that's awesome, but to what extent? If a bunch of people begin to say that traffic lights are a ploy to turn us all into mindless sheeple, or drunk driving is okay, or I can just say and do anything I want because freedom, what the hell kind of world does that look like? It's completely insane. Not all opinions are created equally. Opinions should be formed based on facts, evidence, empathy, and compassion, not what you want to be true or were misled to believe.

I don't fault teachers for not teaching the sort of things I have wound up teaching. Some administrations are overbearing, a lot of people aren't as politically minded, and the dawn of the information age and the internet itself is still relatively new. But I do think for the sake of the sanity and well-being of this country we have got to begin making these points to our children in public schools.

In Luke Savage's column in *Jacobin* called *Liberals Still Think Fact Checking Will Stop the Right. They're Wrong*, after criticizing David Plouffe's book *A Citizen's Guide to Beating Donald Trump*, a book predicated upon the notion that voting and fact-checking conservatives online will beat the right wing, Savage concludes,

> But conservatism is ultimately a political project, not a malign information system. Most people with hardened conservative beliefs won't be swayed by an article from the Wall Street Journal or a Glenn Kessler column giving the birther conspiracy five Pinocchio's – even when it clearly contradicts their stated view. A fact, by itself, is nothing until it becomes part of a larger narrative – and it's these, by and large, that actually structure political identity. In this respect, the Right's willingness to embrace populist storytelling matters a whole lot more than the obvious untruths so regularly put to work in its service. Which is all to say, if we're actually serious about rolling back conservative dominance, fact-checking will never be a substitute for politics.

Conservatism and corporatism is a political project and it's welded against the interest of teachers and the student body alike. It is high time not only to teach students about media literacy, critical thinking, fact-checking, etc. but also to teach them how power itself works in this country, how corporate media shifts the narrative in its favor, and so much more. We're *public* schools after all, are we supposed to join the incessant push for privatization? Or sit back and say nothing while ruthless individualism and incessant privatization eats this country alive? Are we supposed to work to maintain a world where so many American families live paycheck to paycheck just so one of our students in decades of teaching hits the jackpot to become a millionaire or billionaire? Or strive for a more prosperous world? The answers to these questions are obvious. It's time to take our schools back and educate our kids to become thoughtful, empathetic, compassionate, and engaged citizens who contemplate and act upon their own self-interests.

Chapter 4

January – Fake News and the Internet

After looking at what decent journalism *should* look like, we spend the second semester investigating what information we consume every day *actually* looks like as we focus on media literacy. I start by posing a couple of familiar-sounding questions:

Where do you obtain information?

How do you know what is safe to trust?

The answers to these similar questions from the first semester produce some much better answers than the first time around. Even after the first semester focusing on the basics of journalism, kids are a little more confident in their ability to find decent sources and a little less intimidated by the grotesque heap of content in their faces all of the time.

After a group discussion regarding these questions, I show them a picture that has circulated on social media for years: a cartoon of two characters standing on either side of a symbol that could be read as either a "6" or a "9." Each character claims their perspective is correct. The caption says, "Just because you're right does not mean I am wrong. You just haven't seen life from my side." I follow up by asking a few more questions.

Which one of these characters is correct? How do we know they are correct?

What's the intended message of the caption and the meme itself?

We discuss the picture and the questions as a class. Now, I have seen this very meme shared by adults through the years on various social media platforms, and most of the time its function, in my view, is to validate ignorant and abhorrent views under the guise of "well, we all just have opinions, right? Isn't it great that in America everyone is entitled to their opinion?" Though, of course, there is a message of perspective here, the function of this overarching point seems to be to muddy the waters of discourse and provide equal footing to all opinions, even those that come from a place of ignorance matched up against expert or informed opinion. In short: the message of this meme and random guys you went to high school with challenging the advice of virology experts or climate scientists seems to be essentially the same thing.

The kids mostly nail all of this with limited intervention from me. Of course, the lesson is initially lost on some, but generally speaking the kids at least eventually understand that we simply don't have enough information to determine which one of these guys knows what the symbol on the ground means. Some make up stories about the two guys, but at least that is getting them thinking about differences in perspectives. Of course, different and unique perspectives are something to be celebrated, but when you are trying to find the objective truth about something, we should probably look beyond opinions and perspectives and find the facts. If we really think about it, the bottom line is based on what little information we have; it's likely at least one of these guys is speaking from a place of ignorance and does not have an informed idea as to what they're talking about.

So I show them a second picture I have seen shared many times through the years. It's the same cartoon, but the original message is crossed out and replaced with,

But one of these people is wrong. Maybe someone painted a six or a nine, they need to back up and orient themselves, see if there are any other numbers to align with. Maybe there's a driveway or a building to face, or they can ask someone who actually knows. People having an uninformed opinion about something they don't understand and proclaiming their opinion as being equally valid as fact is what is ruining the world. No one wants to do research, they just want to be right.

Now this updated version has a point, doesn't it? What if one of them painted the number? What if one of them knows for sure it's a sideways symbol and neither a 6 or 9? What if neither one actually has a clue? We don't know enough about the two characters to know who is right, but we can imagine a real life scenario where these two characters could state their arguments or do some decent research and get to the ultimate truth regarding which number (or symbol) was etched in the ground. We can hear arguments and check the facts, but simply listening to whoever has an opinion on this and just pretending everyone is correct cannot possibly produce any meaningful answers about this or other similar situations.

Feelings are not the same thing as facts. Though this attitude has been disingenuously co-opted by the Right they truly seem to be the side with the most to gain from being completely feeling-driven.

Timothy Snyder said in his book *On Tyranny*, "To abandon facts is to abandon freedom. If nothing is true, then no one can criticize power, because there is no basis upon which to do so. If nothing is true then all is spectacle. The biggest wallet pays for the most blinding lights." Again, if something is objectively true, why should it not be fair game to bring up in the classroom? If issues still exist in our world and country today, as they undoubtedly do, why wouldn't high school kids want to know about them? Teachers should not only want to offer this material in our classrooms, but we may very well be *obliged* to discuss these matters. Everyone can have an opinion, but opinions must be rooted in fact or else we are going to continue down the path of alternate reality and disinformation. Perhaps if we instill these values in the masses early, then fact-checking by publications will carry more meaning. Additionally, as

Savage stated in *Jacobin*, left politics in this country need to do a far better job of articulating stories and narratives, instead of merely fact-checking. Public schools can and should offer an avenue for both.

Just look at the climate crisis. We know undoubtedly that human activity is warming the planet. Rather than understanding the basic science behind global warming, the Right has injected the information supply with a bunch of voices that amplify the story they want: that humans don't actually have anything to do with the climate crisis, and if they do there is no actual crisis and it's not that big of a deal, and if it is a big deal we will figure it out when it starts to really impact the most powerful countries (since of course the people of smaller and poorer regions and countries are already feeling the impacts).

On a smaller scale we saw the same thing during the COVID-19 pandemic. The scientific consensus was well known, but a few fringe doctors (who were either disgraced or think demon sperm is one of the biggest problems plaguing America) told different stories. Anyone who wanted to believe that the virus was all some kind of false flag latched on to what they wanted to believe without facts and evidence because, hey, everyone is entitled to their opinion and everyone is right and America is awesome because opinions are cool. Right? *Right?!*

I believe this is an important lesson because it's a reminder that, though many issues are complex, we can actually get close to the truth if we value facts and evidence opposed to simply another person confirming our bias by relaying the same opinion. Objective reality doesn't get to be disputed because you feel as though it's not right. The best available evidence built on scientific consensus, facts, or evidence, even if unproven, is still the best available evidence. Even if Dr Fauci ends up being wrong about something, or the weatherman gets the weather wrong one day, are they still not both better bets for accurately predicting behavior of viruses and weather than your crazy

Uncle Larry who watches too much Alex Jones?

Communication, memes, and fake news stories

The next thing we need to do up front is to make a point about the changing nature of communication and the spread of information itself.

From cave paintings to carrier pigeons to newspapers, telephones, televisions, and finally the internet, the point is to make sense of that tsunami of content and information that can make us so anxious. An idea or story that would once spread at a snail's pace can now move around the world in a matter of minutes.

What was once one-way communication between journalists and readers with newspapers, radio, and television has become an interactive behemoth where any voice can be amplified if it hits just right.

Think of the implications. Like-minded people from any vantage point are a click away. As Colonel Robert Bateman said, "Once, every village had an idiot. It took the internet to bring them all together." As we look later in the year at cognitive biases and logical fallacies, general human nature ("if it bleeds it leads," for example) coupled with rapid spread of content, and a 24-hour news cycle is quite a lot to take in.

Any idea can gain traction rapidly. Sifting through information and disinformation can be a daunting task. But how do our newsfeeds and the subsequent ads actually work?

In class I use *"Jaron Lanier Fixes the Internet"* from the *New York Times*. He explains quite well how advertisements and even newsfeeds themselves are individually tailored to each user's preferences and desires. What can seem like everyone in the world agreeing with exactly what you think, posting about the same things, is simply a product of an algorithm. If you're the type that engages in things that make you upset, you're going to get a lot of content that makes you mad. It's all to keep you on the platform so Facebook can convince businesses to buy more ads and make the company more money. A far cry away from the days of a page of ads that were not only not tailor-made to each reader but also easily ignored on a dedicated page of the newspaper. The kids understand, if they didn't already, that we're taking a plunge into uncharted waters because they themselves have been suspicious as to how these ads work – a great example is asking them if they have ever gotten a vaping ad on YouTube. Basically, all of their hands go up. They are shocked to find out not a single time have I ever seen one. As a side note, this is also a decent time for a discussion on campaign financing and campaign ads (as Mainers, they saw a whole lot of Susan Collins and Sara Gideon before the 2020 election…but never even heard of progressive Lisa Savage, who also ran).

With the intent on getting into fake news articles (no, Republicans, I don't mean CNN…no, Democrats, I don't mean Fox News…corporate media deserves a separate critique that we examine next month) I find it beneficial to first do a unit on something the kids are quite familiar with: memes.

Vox has a lighthearted and digestible YouTube video on memes called "Why Do Memes Matter?" The video does well introducing how memes came into prominence and falls in line nicely with the points about the rapid spread of information. It also serves as a worthy introduction to the impact of outright fake or misleading information.

I ask my students to get into groups and get ready to put their cross-referencing media savvy to the test by showing them a few memes and challenging them to determine their validity. The first is a picture of Donald Trump with the quote, "'If I were to run, I'd run as a Republican. They're the dumbest group of voters in the country. They believe anything on Fox News. I could lie and they'd still eat it up. I bet my numbers would be terrific.' – Donald Trump – People Magazine, 1998."

Let's face it, younger people don't like Trump. Many are

inclined to believe this meme. Hell, since 2015, including recently, I have seen this thing shared absent-mindedly by grown adults who somehow missed the many times this quote was debunked within the last several years. But once they cross reference what they are seeing using the tools from this class so far, they realize quickly that, as nice as this fodder would have been to use against their conservative friend, it's simply not true.

Another one I show them targets Hillary Clinton. It says, "Hi, I'm Seth Rich. I was the DNC staffer who gave Wikileaks the DNC emails proving that they had rigged the primaries against Bernie Sanders for Hillary Clinton. Soon after, I was shot twice in the back and killed. Police are still looking for my murderer and Hillary Clinton invokes my name in calling for gun control."

As we now know, Seth Rich somehow went from a low-level staffer to high up in the Clinton campaign after he was tragically and randomly murdered, as even reputable publications played into the shadowy narrative. His own family wants nothing to do with these conspiracies as reported in multiple publications.

And, of course, it isn't just outlandish memes that can be used to make a point. Other memes with sort of half-truths can also be used to show that memes themselves are incredibly small snippets of information and will obviously fail to get in depth when it comes to nuances and complexities about any given issue.

But getting back to the two 2016 candidates who were disparaged via memes during the contentious election that brought us Donald Trump, I would say another point should be made here in terms of selecting candidates. This sort of fake news is not only lazy, but I would argue it's also oppressive. When we're pretending Trump said a bunch of nonsense he didn't really say, we're not paying attention to the absurd things he did say, or more importantly to the policy proposals he had floated or enacted. If we're pretending Hillary Clinton had Seth Rich killed, we're losing sight of her war mongering, allegiance to corporate America, and the true nefarious behavior of the DNC against Sanders. There are worthy grievances to be made about literally any politician, but making things up is lazy and counterproductive. As a side note, some may argue that making this point should come with a "Mr Shain Opinion Alert" as I tend to do when I relay my opinion, but what kind of a teacher would I be if I was partisan? What kind of a teacher would I be if I said, "be completely loyal to your party"? In an age of tribalism for Trump and "blue no matter who" it seems poignant to encourage young people to be critical of our leaders and government instead of becoming good little partisan cheerleaders. And, again, refraining from making this point I would argue would be essentially siding with the Washington elite. The more we know about our political system and the candidates the better we will be able to impact politics to our own benefit.

* * *

Moving from memes to fake news articles and headlines, we take a look at the difference in coverage from random websites that lack credibility and the mainstream media narrative.

While teaching this unit in January 2020, coverage of Kobe Bryant's sudden and tragic death compared to the articles we see surface once in a while that claim Paul Rudd, Betty White, or some other celebrity died when in reality they didn't, created a great illustration.

The day Kobe died I posted on social media, "It's interesting how everyone comes together to trust the news/objective reality when the story has no bearing on politics." A bunch of people were pissed that I didn't say "RIP Kobe," but a few months later millions of people refused to do the small task of wear a mask in public because they believe the media when a celebrity dies but not when there are political implications such as amid a pandemic, or in dealing with the climate crisis, or in knowing the winner of the presidential election. To me this point is worth noting because it's 100 percent true: there is no conspiracy theory that Kobe might still be alive (though I suppose we have seen this sort of thing with Tupac, for example, but I would argue that is more harmless than manipulating opinion on policies that actually impact people's lives), it is just accepted that the basketball legend passed in an untimely fashion because in this case the news was trusted.

But then there's actual fake news that fabricates out of thin air that [insert celebrity here] died just to gain clicks and shares. The book *LikeWar – The Weaponization of Social Media* by PW Singer and Emerson T Brooking reports that in 2016, 59 percent of all links posted on social media had never been clicked on by the person who shared them. This shows pretty clearly that large swaths of people are pacified solely by headlines and by content they already believed. Pointing this out in a negative light hopefully gets kids thinking about their own potential role in perpetuating disinformation.

We look at several fake news stories together in class, starting with satirical websites and then move into sources that take themselves seriously even though the information they publish is questionable. The kids observe that actually clicking links is quite helpful – some of the websites state clearly that the content is satire, which can, of course, become lost on people that are just looking for any headline that would indicate the politician they hate really does suck as they suspected going in. In October 2020, President Trump, for example, actually posted a Babylon Bee article either completely unaware it was satire (he wrote a caption that took the article seriously) or was intentionally trying to mislead people with satire.

Snopes, despite the noted issues with fact checkers as covered earlier, has a collection of fake news stories. Everything from Nancy Pelosi getting hammered at a White House dinner to Colin Kaepernick lobbying to get the National Anthem banned from football, there are a lot of interesting stories to take a look at and show students what overtly fake news stories look like. People love confirming their bias, so it's better to teach students how to be healthy media consumers, as Oxford Internet Institute pointed out all the way back in 2009:

> Our bodies are programmed to consume fats and sugars because they're rare in nature...In the same way, we're biologically programmed to be attentive to things that stimulate: content that is gross, violent, sexual, and that [sic] gossip which is humiliating, embarrassing, or offensive. If we're not careful, we're going to develop the psychological equivalent of obesity. We'll find ourselves consuming content that is least beneficial for ourselves or society as a whole.

Quite true I would say, and scary that this warning was written so long ago apparently to no avail. This is precisely why we need this material covered in schools immediately. It has only gotten worse since 2009 and there's no reason to believe this will slow down on its own.

Before we move on to other forms of fake news and begin the assignment for this unit, we spend some time going over some helpful tools from the Center of Media Literacy by viewing the Five Key Questions of Media Literacy:

Who created this message?

What creative techniques are used to attract my attention?

How might different people understand this message differently than me?

What values, lifestyles, and points of view are represented in, or omitted from, this message?

Why is this message being sent?

The Five Core Concepts from the same Center are also helpful, especially as a bit of foreshadowing for the corporate media unit:

All media messages are "constructed".

Media messages are constructed using a creative language with its own rules.

Different people experience the same media message differently.

Media have embedded values and points of view.

Most media messages are organized to gain profit/and or power.

As a final in-class activity, we read a widely-shared article by NaturalNews.com featuring the headline, "NASA admits that climate change occurs because of changes in Earth's solar orbit, and NOT because of SUVs and fossil fuels."

We read the article, which is chalked full of snazzy images, in class together. It references legitimate sources of information, is decently-written, and doesn't explicitly say it's satire right on the website. It's a bit tougher to identify as fake news because the site presents itself as serious journalism, so we do the cross-referencing and fact-checking together. We saw the source itself, and even the specific story, debunked by multiple websites (NBC, Daily Beast, Snopes, Forbes, etc.) and of course by NASA itself. Afterwards, I break the students into groups so they can answer the Five Key Questions of Media Literacy.

1. Who created this message?

Ethan Huff in *Natural News* – *not* a conventional publication that prides itself on getting the facts correct, correcting itself if it is wrong, or relying on a reputation of journalistic integrity. Huff also suggests corroborating his story with another fringe publication he writes for called *Climate Science News* – this circular approach is not exactly what I meant by cross-referencing last semester. Mike Adams, the creator of Natural News, is a "birther," a 9/11 "truther," an anti-vaxxer who possesses fringe beliefs that object to the entire medical establishment, the government, and conventional wisdom in general. This alone doesn't make any particular claim he says inherently wrong, but it does call into question the creator of the source itself.

2. What creative techniques are used to attract my attention?

Graphics, catchy headline, click bait, the colorful language trying to disparage people who believe the science behind the climate crisis.

3. How might different people understand this message differently than me?

They'll think it's real. Take it all as fact. Distrust in NASA (government) or mainstream media. It could cause deeper entrenchment of beliefs. This sort of information also lends itself to going down rabbit holes where every related anti-government, paranoid conspiracy theory also seems plausible. The idea that Mike Adams has all of the answers while the FDA, government, doctors, scientists, etc. are all out to get us might be possible, but seems unlikely, especially when Adams's solution seems to be to read his publication and buy his vitamins.

4. What values, lifestyles, and points of view are represented in, or omitted from, this message?

No legitimate or recent sources. They completely omit NASA's current actual explanation of climate change and cherry-pick other things that NASA may or may not have said about other matters to craft their own story. The link is there to satisfy people who deny the climate crisis.

5. Why is this message being sent?

Perhaps for *Natural News* to make some money off of ads or to sell supplements and vitamins. They sow distrust in the government and health establishment in general and occupy the space of alternate remedies. Fossil fuel companies would have a lot to gain by claiming their activity isn't contributing to the problem. Sow distrust for media/government.

The fifth Core Concept, "Most media messages are organized to gain profit or power," is worth discussing in detail. On whose behalf is a media source attempting to gain power? The people, the working masses, or corporate America, billionaires, and powerful people who already hold all of the power? Is the source there to question and hold the powerful accountable, or preserve power where it currently exists? Since every purveyor of information is going to have bias, I recommend to the kids to understand their own self-interests and try to consume information that attempts to gain power on their behalf as regular working-class people. Discussing this point also serves as foreshadowing for the corporate media unit, who also operate to gain profit from ads and preserve power for the corporations who buy their ad space and the parties they cheer on. Operating for profit, just as gaining power, is not inherently bad, but it's worth investigating what sort of power the message or messenger is after and in what fashion they are profiting. Additionally, does the profit come from corporations buying ads or from the readers themselves? Writers and journalists have to eat – but who is paying them, and how does it affect the reporting and content?

Another interesting point is that *Natural News*, like Alex Jones and *InfoWars*, is actually banned from Facebook. This is a wonderful time, particularly as we saw the president himself banned from social media services at the end of his presidency after the riot at the Capitol over delusional and anti-democracy premises, to discuss whether or not private tech companies should be banning websites or figures. Getting kids to think about where that line should be drawn, or if it should be drawn at all by unelected and unaccountable tech moguls, is a wonderful conversation to have. Suggesting how things might be different if Facebook was nationalized is also a great part of the discussion – I suspect if it were operated in the public sector, governed differently, and didn't exist to keep us addicted and mine our data, social media might actually improve significantly. Additionally, discussing the fate of Parler, a right-wing social media site that claimed to be an ardent supporter of free speech, was essentially eliminated for a time when it was removed from the big app stores. This discussion is an important one to have with young people as we venture into the uncharted waters of social media and their role in the world.

After a thorough investigation into fake news (or as thorough as we can be with so much to cover in so little time) it's time to break things up with a graded assignment: write your own fake news story.

The students are free to put out any sort of disinformation they like. The only catch is for the second part of the assignment they must explain why their fake news story might be successful, what kind of agenda it pushes, what sort of damage it might do if it became widely accepted or went viral, who or what stands to gain power from it, etc.

Though it might seem counterintuitive to have kids write their own version of the thing I am cautioning about, I think it's a solid way to approach this for a few reasons. First, the kids have fun with it. They like to be able to have the freedom to make something up and be a little mischievous. Second, the point can be made after they write these stories that anyone can write this stuff and post it online. If they had a somewhat-polished webpage and the right people found it and shared it in their online communities, their own version of nonsensical fake news stories could go viral in a heartbeat. Finally, the second portion of the assignment forces them to think about their own fake news and the problems therein.

Identifying fake news, they will soon see, is the easy part. February has something much more tricky in store: juxtaposing the issues of outright lying in fake news with the manufactured consent we see via mainstream corporate media. This material I would say is somewhat advanced for high school kids, but a critique of the mainstream corporate media, especially as we've been touting it for cross-referencing and fact-checking purposes to this point, is critical in developing an understanding of information, how it is passed, and how it relates to power, politics, and parties today and beyond.

Chapter 5

February/March – Corporate Media

Most Americans suspect there is something wrong with mainstream corporate media. Whether it's apolitical people shutting off the news entirely, Republicans distrustful of CNN, MSNBC, or the *NY Times*, Democrats realizing Fox News is not really a news network, or leftists realizing that any corporate network is going to come with inherent flaws because media corporations operate primarily for profit, not necessarily to meaningfully inform, most Americans realize media is highly imperfect and often comes with an agenda of its own. The problem is far too often critiques of American corporate media are misguided and belligerent.

It seems quite obvious at this point that without adequate and honest discussion on media in schools people end up finding all sorts of explanations for the way the world works in other places. Whether they stumble into independent sources like Prager U, *Jacobin*, or random cranks on YouTube, it seems that a thorough and in-depth critique of mainstream media is necessary. Without one, as we have seen first-hand, media narratives about a pandemic, for example, are dismissed out of hand. Conspiracy theories and propaganda fill the void and we drown in a sea of ignorance and confusion.

Without developing a certain lens for corporate media viewing, we end up with a population that either takes on an irrationally faithful belief of everything that their certain corporate sources peddle (which as we will see is often along party lines and doesn't really leave room for the shared flaws of both parties), or it leaves them trusting fringe or conspiratorial versions of a story which generally lacks evidence and facts.

Of course, the truth is, like many things these days, we

should view corporate media with a skeptical eye, but not lazily dismiss and ignore their reporting entirely. If they report a celebrity died, it's very likely the celebrity actually did die. If they report that according to experts tracking the virus, a pandemic has killed a bunch of people and a good way to prevent the spread of a virus, according to the CDC and WHO, is to socially distance and wear a mask as evident with other countries like Japan who did so, while there may be undue emphasis or voices omitted, it isn't the same thing as fake news.

It's a really tricky thing to teach because I don't want to leave my students becoming distrustful of everything the media says. This isn't the point, which I impress upon my students throughout the corporate media unit. I certainly do not want students conflating CNN or even Fox News, even with its flaws and extremely dangerous propaganda, to satirical websites or outright nonsensical sources. But as we know the media doesn't always get everything right. Look at the selling of the Iraq War. Notice the lack of diversity in voices from a class and economic standpoint. Observe how by nature cable news works in soundbites and snippets rather than substance. Acknowledge the emphasis on culture wars and omission of a story like Steven Donziger, the American lawyer who successfully sued Chevron for dumping toxic waste on the Ecuadorian rainforest, was sued by Chevron, and then placed under house arrest for an unprecedented amount of time. See what happens to coverage within a partisan network when a new administration enters the White House, when advertisers need to be satisfied, when ideas or people receive flak, or when the finger is pointed at a common enemy that distracts from a broader story. Two wonderful works to use for this unit are *Manufacturing Consent* by Edward Herman and Noam Chomsky as well as *Hate Inc.* by Matt Taibbi.

Using Manufacturing Consent and Hate Inc. in the classroom

Manufacturing Consent is an older book and a dense read. Its lessons are important, but high school kids struggle with paying attention and setting aside time to read for a class, and a book like *Manufacturing Consent* is likely too cumbersome for most high school students.

A wonderful video produced by *Al Jazeera* and narrated by *Democracy Now*'s Amy Goodman is an accessible tool for passing Herman and Chomsky's Five Filters of Mass Media to high school students. Concisely explained with captivating animation, the video lays out the Five Filters of Mass Media: Ownership, Advertising, Media Elite, Flak, and Common Enemy. *The Listening Post* also has a full interview with Chomsky, Taibbi, and other journalists discussing *Manufacturing Consent* a bit more in depth. I highly recommend pausing frequently and rephrasing and providing some quick examples during the video, as well as checking for understanding and opening the floor for questions.

After the students have a very general understanding of the filters, it's important to illustrate the filters by connecting them to real issues and coverage. There are loads of examples to use for each filter, here are a few I happen to use:

Ownership – Some readers may remember a few years ago a video circulated on social media featuring a slew of local news anchors around the country repeating the same exact spiel about how biased news is "plaguing the country" and is a "threat to democracy." The reason a bunch of seemingly unconnected local news anchors all repeated the same script is because they are all owned by Sinclair Broadcasting, a right-wing media company that owns nearly 300 local stations (two, as I point out, here in Maine – WGME and WPFO).

Anyone who sees this is taken back. Without any sort of context, I even saw Trump supporters sharing the video as though to say, "wow, look at the fake news media" even though the mechanical news anchors were a product of a right-wing entity. It's overtly alarming when you first see it, and without any sort of context it just sows distrust in all sorts of mainstream networks, so it's worth taking a deeper dive.

PBS News Hour has a great YouTube video on the subject called "How Sinclair Broadcasting puts a partisan tilt on trusted local news." This is helpful because it points out that a network, even if it appears folksy and local, can actually be owned by a larger corporation with a different agenda than merely providing local news. That particular corporation may very well have a specific agenda and actively spin different narratives to viewers that would be advantageous to the corporation's interests beyond simply getting news out to people. As we see throughout this unit, selling advertising and protecting the interests of advertisers and gaining clicks can leave decent journalism and worthwhile information ignored. Furthermore, seemingly innocuous local coverage sees editorials sprinkled in nationwide by former member of the Trump administration Boris Epshteyn. Since the Fairness Doctrine was overturned in the 80s, networks are no longer required to give equal time to opposing views. This allowed Rush Limbaugh and Rupert Murdoch to spout messages of privatization, authoritarianism, and corporatized economics with no opposition, as CNN and MSNBC later followed suit. As all of these networks convince millions of Americans to believe narratives that objectively go against their own self-interests, power itself solidifies and compounds.

The Five Key Questions of Media Literacy also, of course, play a role here: who created a message on, for example, Maine's WGME? Well, right-wing media Sinclair Broadcasting, that's who. And when we bear in mind rule number 5 of the Five Core Concepts of Media, many media messages are designed to gain profit or power, not relinquish it if a story is inconvenient for the big owners.

Advertising – Teachers can illustrate the advertising filter by discussing the experience all of us have on social media sites like Instagram, Facebook, or YouTube. As explained in those lessons, we users of the seemingly-free service are actually the product sold to the advertiser – and corporate media is no different in this way. We are sucked into the TV or the media outlet with the expectation that we will see the advertisements on the outlet and spend our money accordingly. Of course, anyone who fancies themselves as a free thinker scoffs at the notion that anyone could possibly be influenced by some obnoxious advertisement, but advertising wouldn't be a $700 billion a year industry if it didn't work on some level.

This opens the door to a separate point about ad-free or paid services. An example kids can relate to is a Netflix subscription when compared to YouTube, or a Spotify premium account when compared to the free platform. You pay to use the services free from ads, and sometimes news can be viewed in a similar way. Of course, this opens up another door in discussing if reliable, decent information should be more accessible, and how the role of free and more accessible media can shape public opinion while more substantial information could be locked behind a paywall at times. It should be pointed out that poor people who can't afford to spend extra money on reliable news sources should also have a right to factual information as well if we are going to run a functioning democracy. Though worthy of discussion, these are incredibly broad and complex questions that are worth mentioning but that we don't have a ton of time for with everything else we need to discuss.

Anyway, how does the profit-motive and advertising affect reporting? It's not enough to point out that you're going to have to suffer through annoying ads when you consume what appears at a glance to be free media. We must consider how the presence and necessity of advertisers within this business model may actually wind up dictating what is or isn't reported, or how a story, or campaign, is covered.

Just look at Donald Trump in 2016. Here's CBS CEO Leslie Moonves on Trump's rise and how it affected his network as reported by *Hollywood Reporter*:

> "It may not be good for America, but it's damn good for CBS," he said of the presidential race.
>
> Moonves called the campaign for president a "circus" full of "bomb throwing," and he hopes it continues.
>
> "Man, who would have expected the ride we're all having right now?...The money's rolling in and this is fun," he said.
>
> "I've never seen anything like this, and this is going to be a very good year for us. Sorry. It's a terrible thing to say. But, bring it on, Donald. Keep going," said Moonves.
>
> "Donald's place in this election is a good thing," he said.

Trump, a former reality show star, knows how to capture attention, so CBS and Moonves knew airing him all of the time would gain clicks and views and cause advertisers to want to spend at CBS, or any other network with nonstop coverage that isn't necessarily intelligent or meaningful. It may not inform, but boy does it entertain. Sure, it might not be good for America, but it's awesome for CBS. This sort of free coverage for Trump frankly makes Russia's efforts pale in comparison (more on that later) and is a poignant example of how a successful enterprise within a capitalist system may be extremely profitable for a handful of people but detrimental to the greater good.

Since we've already picked on Republicans, let's look at the other right-wing American entity, Democrats. Corporate media couldn't have been more delighted with oligarch Mike Bloomberg's vanity campaign that ABC News reported spent over $1 billion of his own money during his 100-day campaign. Well over half of that total was spent on cable, broadcast, and radio alone. The Democratic Party itself bent the rules just to allow Bloomberg a late entry into the race. A Trump vs. Bloomberg hypothetical may not have left any hope for democracy or the American people with two billionaires duking it out, but it sure would have been great for advertising revenue.

Or how about when Bernie Sanders on live television during a 2019 debate called out CNN for disingenuous framing ("how do we pay for it?") of his Medicare for All proposal by correctly pointing out that Big Pharma would be advertising on the debate that night? Low and behold he was correct. Though it is unspoken, can we not safely surmise that if CNN began to tout the Sanders campaign (rather than, like other corporate networks whose interests Sanders' proposals do not jive with, do their best to ignore or disparage the campaign as they did in both 2016 and 2020) that these types of advertisers would simply take their money elsewhere?

Sludge reported in early 2020 that 94 percent of Comcast Executives gave generously to the Joe Biden campaign. The same article also cites a *Columbia Journalism Review* study that found Biden received far more positive coverage from Comcast's MSNBC. The article went on:

An analysis of MSNBC transcripts from August and September by In These Times that looked at how often Sanders, Biden and Sen. Elizabeth Warren were mentioned and the tone of the coverage produced similar findings. "Over the two months, these six programs focused on Biden, often to the exclusion of Warren and Sanders," In These Times found. "Sanders received not only the least total coverage (less than one-third of Biden's), but the most negative."

The same article reported, "Despite his campaign's viral grassroots energy – observable at his rallies and through his fundraising figures – Sanders was excluded from graphics and his polling and fundraising numbers were misreported in ways that made his campaign look less successful than it was."

And in the spirit of transparency both in this book and in the classroom, I volunteered about 10 hours a week for a few months between teaching and taking classes to obtain my teaching certification as a Bernie Victory Captain in 2020, and I also volunteered in 2016 (or as I like to think of it, volunteering not necessarily for Bernie Sanders, but a broader leftist project). As I explained to my kids that year, this is because I, as one of the many teachers who fueled the Sanders campaign, believe that his proposals were in my own best interest. I defy anyone who says that participating in civic engagement and identifying the candidate who best suits my interests as a voter is something that should be left out of the classroom. Saying that type of point should be off limits in classrooms couldn't delight the powers that be more. If they wind up thinking that unbridled free market capitalism may suit their interests better than Sanders-type proposals, that's fine, but at least they're thinking in depth about what they want out of their candidate instead of buying into bland soundbites and partisan tribalism.

The examples of reporting running through Herman and Chomsky's first two filters couldn't be more obvious. Showing students that advertising and ownership inherently affect media coverage, and consequently elections and by extension democracy itself, is not only important but it also further illustrates a main theme in this book that bias is becoming ever-obvious if you actually take the time to analyze what is being said. Through omission and emphasis anything can be biased, so we should not only be teaching kids how to spot bias, but giving them a variety of things to think about so they can develop their own opinions and learn how to strive for their own self-interests as civically-engaged Americans. Absolutely none of this is meant to re-litigate past elections, what's done is done. But these examples not only serve as a different way of viewing elections beyond the bland partisan status quo, but are also perfect examples of the filters as described in *Manufacturing Consent*. I monitored the 2016 and 2020 elections quite closely, so I am able to go in depth on these matters with students should questions arise. If you're a teacher reading this, perhaps you will come up with other examples of ownership and advertising. Furthermore, as I have argued here, we must begin to openly teach from the left on behalf of the working-class masses; as historian Thomas Frank has written and spoken about extensively, populist movements always face backlash from the ruling elite, including the media.

The populist movements of the late 1800s as well as Franklin Roosevelt's New Deal dealt with massive opposition via the media. A world and country that moves beyond many of the crises we face today will require a populist movement that can see beyond this type of propaganda opposing sensible populist movements like the Sanders insurgency.

Media elite & flak – More and more Americans are figuring out that the whole story isn't being told in the media. This hunch can manifest in ways both good and bad. Through an intelligent lens, we can consume corporate media and its narratives with a skeptical eye and still get a great deal of solid information from them, but if the rightful hunch about media runs amok and isn't done thoughtfully, bogus conspiracy theories tend to take the place of factual sources – but more on that later.

As we see frequently, and as Matt Taibbi brilliantly explains in *Hate Inc.*, there are certain stories that aren't acceptable because they challenge shortcomings regarding our government which leave both parties complicit. When we analyze something like bloated military spending while other public institutions crumble, new ideas are written off as "we can't afford it" while trillions are spent on perpetual military conflict, imperialism, tax breaks for the wealthy, and corporate subsidies, none of these are convenient stories for the partisan cheerleaders in media because both sides are guilty, so that entire narrative goes under-reported – or probably more likely, completely ignored by corporate media.

Although Bernie Sanders ultimately ended up siding with the establishment yet again, his campaign was difficult for corporate media to cover because it was in many ways an indictment of both corporatist parties. This is why the media and the establishment tried their best to ignore the campaign in 2016 and were openly against it in 2020. Sadly, this isn't hyperbole but a reality, which is why the Sanders ordeal makes such a timely and accurate example when teaching *Manufacturing Consent*.

In October 2019 Sanders had the biggest rally of the primary season in New York City. Photographs showed a sea of people, a massive visual spectacle, but the *NY Times* tossed that on page A29 of the print edition, and the online edition shared to social media featured a picture of Alexandria Ocasio-Cortez, who spoke at the event, not pictured giving a speech to the masses but instead seen in a stock image, sitting on a leather couch indoors somewhere. Imagine for a moment if any of the other establishment picks held such a rally. Considering the same paper showed Amy Klobuchar lecturing to a dozen people at some town hall, I have a feeling the coverage would have been different.

Then there's columnists and reporters who create narratives such as Jennifer Rubin, who went from writing the column "Why Iowa is so important to Democratic candidates running for president" to asking "What good are the Iowa caucuses anyway?" in a column once Sanders surged into the lead. We also saw unfounded claims about "Bernie Bros," the idea that Sanders's base was white male 20-somethings even though we found out from more honest sources (*Vice*, for example, had coverage on this) that this was factually inaccurate. Even worse, incoherent, and devoid of evidence, the corporate media actually claimed without a shred of evidence that Sanders' supporters were somehow meaner or "more toxic" than fans of other candidates.

We saw the media throw up all sorts of other Hail Mary's to "stop Sanders." The Elizabeth Warren story about how Sanders supposedly said a woman couldn't be president can be debunked by viewing a video of Sanders in 1988 saying a woman can be president, along with the fact he asked her to run in 2016 – the only reason Sanders ended up running is because Warren declined the suggestion. Then there's the incoherent claims of Sanders' apparent lack of "electability" which haplessly ignored the failed strategy of 2016 and blatantly disregarded polling that showed Sanders did the best with independent voters and was also poised to beat Trump in a general election.

Or how about, with absolutely not a single shred of evidence, on the eve of the Nevada Caucus when all corporate media sources played the Russia card against Sanders? Granted, it didn't end up working as he became the first candidate to win the popular vote in the first three primaries, but yet still they tried. Considering Hillary Clinton was picked as the winner before primaries even started in 2016, I think it's fair to surmise not only would the Democratic media arms not have worked overtime to blast an establishment figure after they became the first candidate to win the first three primaries, but they would have likely demanded other candidates, especially insurgents, drop out to "back the blue."

But, of course, the Nevada eve smear didn't work, so people like Chris Matthews openly spooked his audience into a frenzy by claiming the Sanders surge was akin to a Nazi invasion, and it would mean executions would occur in Central Park. We saw increased red baiting in corporate media. The establishment even openly considered disregarding the democratic process and drafting Sherrod Brown if Sanders won the nomination. By the end of February there were stories coming out, even in the

NY Times, about party insiders openly trying to "stop Sanders," and a few days later we saw the establishment coalesce around a mentally-slipping neoliberal with a career-conservative voting record and literally zero volunteer or ground game anywhere due to lack of enthusiasm – and we also know that the Democrat darling Barack Obama, who has clearly *never* been a friend of progressives or leftists, was instrumental in making that happen.

As a former student of mine said on Facebook, "it's like the DNC would rather lose with Biden than win with Bernie." While Bernie was questioned about praising Cuban literacy programs back in the 80s, corporate media did very little to question Biden about his repeated lying during the one-on-one debate between the two of them, let alone a career spent getting "tough on crime" or trying to gut social security. And despite the #MeToo movement, Biden's strange tendencies to sniff women and the allegation by Tara Reade was generally ignored in corporate media; ignored, unbelievably, while Sanders was incoherently and disingenuously accused of being a misogynist no less. The flak and smearing of America's most popular senator, who I believe would have destroyed Trump one on one, was all to prevent things like Medicare for All, the Green New Deal, and a progressive wealth tax, at the demand of the wealthy corporations who buy ads on these corporate networks. If this isn't a clear example of "flak," I don't know what is.

As great as this illustration is, for some tastes it might be "too soon" to discuss the 2016 and 2020 Democratic Primaries so I will give a few other examples, beginning with the Jon Stewart appearance on CNN's *Crossfire* from back in 2004.

Discussing the political landscape with Republican Tucker Carlson and Democrat Paul Begala, Stewart, the lone guest on a show that usually featured two other partisans, took both "partisan hacks" (as he called them on air) to task for dishonest and fluffy political coverage. Though he often can't get to his main points because Carlson in particular is a master at redirecting the conversation, Stewart was making the point that corporate media outlets and their talking heads were nothing more than partisan cheerleaders – a far cry from what the press should do in holding the powerful accountable, digging for information, and informing the public. The kids also enjoy this clip because it gets a little heated and uncomfortable. It's also interesting to point out that Stewart's appearance actually was a big reason why the show was canceled shortly thereafter. Stewart and Sanders both exposed which entities have greater access and favor in the eyes of corporate media.

Issues that are substantive and bipartisan are the finest examples to use in explaining media elite and flak. These two filters show the sliver of acceptable opinion. As Taibbi notes, journalists these days live in cities and often subsequently possess a corresponding worldview. How often do we hear from workers in columns anymore? What about a Marxist or anarchist getting a regular op-ed in the pages of the *NY Times*, or even a blue-collar Trump supporter or union organizer? How about an activist?

When we go back to something like militarism, this is a bipartisan consensus that America like clockwork just drops hundreds of billions of dollars every year on imperialism with zero "how do we pay for it?" pushback. It's not covered in the news, and people who want to talk about it get flak. Again, this isn't an exaggeration at all: every year any program that benefits working people is written off as "too expensive" and "we can't afford it" while we spend over one trillion dollars annually on militarism, corporate subsidies, and tax breaks for the wealthy, and corporate media *never, ever* says "we can't afford it." Congress is so against doing anything helpful for working-class people that even in the middle of a pandemic, financial relief for the working class or better healthcare was out of the question while big corporations got bailed out and massive military budgets signed off on without any scrutiny from the mainstream corporate press.

Another couple of examples that work well in this unit are two interviews on Neil Cavuto's show on Fox News. In the first, young organizer Keely Mullen goes on to talk with Cavuto about student loan forgiveness. She is clearly unprepared, takes a great amount of flak, and is in no position to defend herself. The video was viewed over 2 million times because conservatives see it as an honest debate with the wise conservative Cavuto dominating the young and naive "socialist."

But Cavuto later had a worthier opponent in Darletta Scruggs. Cavuto, of course, isn't being a journalist when he has these young women on, he is not asking unbiased questions, he is blatantly peddling questions within a right-wing framework, throwing in right-wing talking points, and all the while presenting as an objective journalist on a news network. It's not an interview, it's a debate. Scruggs, unlike Mullen, came prepared to deliver her answers and frankly Cavuto had no real answer for her. Cavuto could not answer questions from his young guest that dealt with how he claims we "can't afford" public college or healthcare but, like every other conservative, never says anything about debt and spending when it comes to wars, corporate subsidies, and tax breaks. He tried to give her flak by conducting the entire interview from a right-wing vantage point, but she held her own and battled back. Not only is this clip illustrative of the point, but it's inspiring for the students to see a younger person taking the older "journalist" to task.

And finally, if you dare, teachers, RussiaGate is another prime example of a media elite narrative, and an example of corporate media gone completely haywire. We heard for literally years that Donald Trump and Russia colluded, that Trump was something akin to a secret agent or something. I saw countless people on my social media thinking any day would be "Mueller time" and Trump would be removed from office in handcuffs because he was "Putin's puppet."

Yet absolutely zero evidence was produced to prove collusion. Some Democrats still like to think of Russia as this extremely scary boogeyman because they "meddled in our election" and tried to "upend democracy." For the love of God, look at the ads Russia took out. Show students the *NY Times* article, "These Are the Ads Russia Bought on Facebook in 2016," which floats the idea that such ads "tipped the scales for Trump in 2016." Let the students figure out if such content really did "tip the scales." Memes of Jesus and Satan arm wrestling, random points all over the political spectrum – the idea that Russia was the factor that tipped the scales, and not guys like Rupert Murdoch's Fox News or Moonves CBS, or even general economic and social unrest and a US population tired of the status quo, is utterly asinine. The idea that America, which has not only administered its own disinformation campaigns at home and abroad, but literally toppled entire governments and installed its own figures around the world, is the one under attack is laughable. The entire "RussiaGate" narrative was wonderful in absolving Hillary Clinton of guilt and in letting corporate media pundits off the hook for doing such a bad job calling the 2016 election, but its claims simply did not materialize. Rather than a legitimate critique of explanation of the demagogue Trump filling the corporate media airwaves, we got a glorified spy thriller, fueled by a sense of American exceptionalism. When Mueller failed to prove collusion, Trump came out smelling like a rose – a gift he did not deserve due to coverage that in no way meaningfully informed the public. It was the media elite filter that allowed this story to gain prominence, and it's flak that keeps journalists like Aaron Maté, who did excellent reporting on "RussiaGate," from setting the record straight on corporate outlets.

Common enemy – Finally the most straightforward filter, common enemy. Take your pick for which example to use.

Conservatives use a host of enemies to watch out for from immigrants to terrorists to Muslim people to the homeless to the welfare recipient, the list goes on and on. Democrats, of course, use Russia, white nationalists, etc. Both parties and their media arms are increasingly doing something I consider quite frightening, which is to point to the members of the other party and fashion them as the common enemy (as I point out to my students, you have more in common with your neighbor who likes the opposite party than you do with the people truly running the world). Both sides also clearly viewed Sanders as a common enemy, as well as any left-leaning socialist ideology or policy proposal – which I believe is less of a reflection on the ideas themselves and more of a reflection on how well mainstream narratives have done in keeping these ideas taboo. With the s-word label removed, people actually agree with "socialism" like Medicare for All, Green New Deal, empowering workers, increased minimum wage (in 2020 the proposal won in Florida where Biden lost), or taxing the wealthy.

Of course, leftists have their own common enemies. Mainly both establishments, corporate America, and of course the government which corporate America controls. The common enemy filter depends on the aim and bias of the source itself – is the source biased in favor of a specific party or a specific set of ideas?

Information of this nature is naturally going to point the finger at someone or something. Americans are increasingly hyper-aware that something is very wrong with this country and how we do things, especially amid the COVID era. Trump ran a campaign built on pointing the finger at all sorts of common enemies, and I don't think this is very surprising since Trump himself is a viewer of Fox News.

Meanwhile, Joe Biden says billionaires and corporate America are not the problem, that Trump is the problem. Most of us on the left view Trump as a symptom of a much larger problem dealing with corporations hoarding wealth, gutting resources, and destroying our environment, but Biden and other establishment Democrats can't point the finger at this common enemy because corporations also fund their campaigns, so they're always stuck pretending as though merely removing Trump or talking nicer would, ironically, magically make America great again.

The point of this filter should not be to pretend like there aren't enemies out there. The point should be to look in depth at various media tropes that don't actually hold water upon close examination: the odds of an undocumented immigrant committing a violent crime. The odds of being killed by a terrorist. An honest look at what Russia actually did during the 2016 election juxtaposed with the over-hyped version people like Rachel Maddow spouted on the news on a nightly basis, or an honest look at what Marxism or socialism actually means.

Hell, the whole unit in itself identifies a common enemy to keep an eye on in consuming corporate media through a sensible lens. The point isn't to be nice to everyone and not identify the entities causing problems in this country, the point should be to examine the played-out media tropes and to investigate some topics that go under-reported because they clash with the previous two filters in media elite and flak. The point isn't to demonize pointing out common enemies, but to think about who is in power, who or what is actually doing damage, and who or what is being used as a dishonest scapegoat.

Other materials and ideas for the corporate media unit

As mentioned, journalist and media critic Matt Taibbi wrote a fantastic contemporary critique of media in *Hate Inc*. It reads in many ways like an updated and modern *Manufacturing Consent*. Similar to Herman/Chomsky's Five Filters, Taibbi uses Ten Rules of Hate to make his points. I highly recommend reading the book, but here are my notes for the kids on the ten rules:

Matt Taibbi says in his book *Hate Inc.* you're not pursuing real political knowledge by consuming corporate media such as CNN, MSNBC, or Fox. The Ten Rules of Hate are similar to the Five Filters of Mass Media – he says powerful people are not going to allow truly revolutionary or dangerous ideas on TV: "The news today is a reality show where you're part of the cast: America vs. America on every channel."

1. THERE ARE ONLY TWO IDEAS – We've discussed the limited spectrum of acceptable opinion, you must connect with one of the two ideas because that's all that's offered on these networks. Dissenting or nuanced points of view will receive flak or outright omission from the airwaves.

2. THE TWO IDEAS ARE IN PERMANENT CONFLICT – Democrats and Republicans endlessly battle as if there is no ideological alternative between their two, often very similar, platforms. While they may agree on military spending, corporate tax breaks, etc. there are always points of disagreement where the two sides can pretend to be polar opposites even though they may actually agree on a multitude of issues, particularly economically, or, as we'll see when we get to our Iraq War unit, with the next war.

3. HATE PEOPLE, NOT INSTITUTIONS – "though most of our problems are systemic, it's more convenient to hate people, not the system itself." Particularly people of the opposite party. "In *Manufacturing Consent*, Chomsky and Herman noted that in the aftermath of our loss in Vietnam we regularly debated the morality of war journalism, but more rarely discussed the apparently less-important subjects like invasion, occupation, bombing civilians, and so on." We see a similar dynamic to the War on Terror. He goes on to relate this to the second filter, advertising: "The biggest outlets learned there's no percentage in doing big exposés against large, litigious companies. Not only will they sue, but they're also certain to pull ads as punishment (this was a big consideration in the Monsanto case,

as Fox and 22 stations that could all have used NutraSweet ads). Why make trouble?" This is a far cry from holding the powerful accountable and informing citizens – this is the media behaving like a PR firm.

4. EVERYTHING IS SOMEONE ELSE'S FAULT – The Fairness Doctrine has been eliminated so we often don't actually hear from the other side. The most attractive stories for a partisan press are those that make the parties seem like two polar opposites ideologically. That way one side is good and the other evil. There's no room for nuance.

Flow chart:

SOMETHING BAD HAPPENS

Can it be blamed on the other party?

YES (we do the story)

NO (we don't do the story- see rule #5)

5. NOTHING IS EVERYONE'S FAULT – If both parties have an equal or near-equal hand in causing a social problem, the corporate media typically won't cover it – more accurately, a reporter or two might cover it, but it's never picked up as a story that dominates the 24-hour news cycle for a substantial period of time. If it doesn't take over a news cycle, it doesn't become "a thing." Examples: bloated military budget, mass surveillance, American support for dictatorships, drone assassination, torture, the drug war, etc. You must look to sources, outlets, and books beyond the corporate-owned news cycle that dare to hold the powerful accountable to gain different perspectives.

6. ROOT DON'T THINK – Just watch a debate. The questions are within the narrative and framework of the corporate network with corporate advertisers, they often do not touch upon something as problematic as the climate crisis at all, and ultimately it's about rooting for your team over policy proposals and things like that. It often looks like WWE or a sports talk show. "This nonsense has had the effect of depoliticizing elections and turning them into blunt contests of tactics, fundraising, and

rhetorical technique...Since our own politicians are typically very disappointing, we particularly root for the other side to lose."

7. NO SWITCHING TEAMS – Begala (the Democrat in the John Stewart Crossfire episode) couldn't say one single nice thing about George W. Bush, demonstrating there is no "fair and balanced" in corporate media as Fox News claimed as their slogan for years. Objectivity is taking a back seat in recent years in journalism and it may never be the same again – it is so important not only to learn bias and know who is giving you your information, but also to develop an understanding and informed-opinions on these issues. "The model going forward will likely involve Republican media covering Democratic corruption and Democratic media covering Republican corruption." This is essentially where we're heading. Being out of touch with what the other side is thinking is no longer seen as a fault because:

8. THE OTHER SIDE IS LITERALLY HITLER – Fox News's Glenn Beck was the OG "the other side is Hitler" guy. In turn, Trump became Hitler even before he was elected.

> If Trump supporters are Hitler, and all liberals are also Hitler, this brings Crossfire to its natural conclusion. The America vs. America show is now Hitler vs. Hitler! Think of the ratings! The new show leaves out 100 million people who didn't vote at all (a group that by itself is nearly as big as both the Clinton and Trump electorates combined), but this is part of the propaganda.

Non-voters are the biggest factor (think of the many reasons why they're not voting) but they're nowhere to be found on TV, "because they suspend our disbelief in the Hitler vs. Hitler show."

9. IN THE FIGHT AGAINST HITLER, EVERYTHING IS

PERMITTED – Don't think about anything complicated, fight "Hitler." Stewart pointed out on Crossfire that the show itself didn't stand for anything, it was just an endless argument of "political theater" and not educational or meaningful to its viewers. Taibbi suggests things could get even more uncivil since each side sees the other as Hitler.

10. FEEL SUPERIOR – "We know you know the news we show you is demeaning, disgusting, pointless, and not really intended to inform." The point of cable news is to get you thinking of the other side or the people covered in stories, "what idiots!" He argues that the people (see Rule #3) ridiculed by the media are used to make us as consumers feel superior, particularly in comparison to figures on "the other side" who corporate media consumers love to hate.

Taibbi concludes the section: "We can't get you there unless you follow the rules. Accept a binary world and pick a side. Embrace the reality of being surrounded by evil stupidity. Feel indignant, righteous, and smart. Hate losers, love winners. Don't challenge yourself. And during commercials, do some shopping. Congratulations, you're the perfect news consumer."

Taibbi's book expands upon some of the ideas from *Manufacturing Consent* and sort of rehashes some of the themes in a different way for a different time. Perhaps Taibbi's Ten Rules will register with a few students more effectively than the Five Filters. Taibbi is a fantastic critic of the news and a voice certainly worth amplifying in a unit like this – particularly since he is still an active journalist doing great work on the campaign trail and on huge issues such as the corporate COVID bailout.

Another great resource for this unit that illustrates the Ten Rules of Hate and the Five Filters in an accessible fashion is the documentary *Outfoxed*. It's a little dated (which again might be more comfortable for some teachers – I very much doubt any feathers will be ruffled when analyzing Fox's coverage of John Kerry back in 2004 for example) but it's a solid documentary that outlines a variety of tactics used not only by Fox, but increasingly by all of the competing major corporate networks now as well. The supposedly "fair and balanced" Fox News was a pioneer in becoming an opinion-based arm of a political party masquerading as honest news, and made a bunch of money doing so. The examples of manufactured consent and dishonest journalism can and should be connected to how the network, as well as MSNBC, CNN, etc., operate to this very day. Unfortunately, this approach to news may not be informative, but it makes a lot of money. Of course, our system only cares about economic growth, not fostering a general well-being of the masses.

Finishing up the corporate media unit

I'll be the first to say this is a hell of a lot to cover for a high school kid in a matter of several weeks. My hope is for a variety of themes to stick. One thing to be very aware of is to make sure that this doesn't turn into an unhealthy distrust of the media. I don't believe we want students equating CNN or Fox News coverage, even despite its obvious shortcomings, to blatantly fake news articles. But we should guide them to developing a healthy skepticism of media narratives.

This has always felt like the opportunity to do an essay. Previously, my assignments have been articles and things like that, but with the media unit I think it's a good time for an essay. Here are my instructions for this assignment (and perhaps you'll have a different idea for your final assignment – though it's not my style, even a test or quiz could potentially work):

Write an essay about what you have learned in class the last few weeks. Some questions to get you started (but certainly think of other things to discuss if you can): What have you learned about problems with mainstream corporate media? What have you learned about consuming information in general? Do you agree the mainstream media manufactures consent? What are a few examples? How does mainstream media compare to online fake news?

If you are stuck on what to write about, the safest direction to go is to discuss the Five Filters of Mass Media. You can discuss each filter in depth, provide examples, explain how you will use this knowledge in your lives, how you will view corporate media through a different lens knowing what you know now. You are essentially showing me what you have learned the past few weeks in class.

Additionally, and you may find this helpful for any English class just as I do, I wrote an essay on essays to help students with the formula of an essay:

Essay On Essays

Essays are an important part of the student experience. High school students should know how to write essays not only for their current classes, but for their secondary education. Essays should follow a basic formula; the introduction, for example, should introduce the topic or argument. As a whole, a properly-written essay should include an introductory paragraph complete with a thesis statement as the last sentence (or two) of the paragraph to describe the point of the essay, at least three body-paragraphs of at least three sentences each, and a conclusion in which the writer summarizes the point of the essay.

Students will use the opening body-paragraph to make their first point. They will decide whether they want to start out with their strongest argument, or perhaps leave that for the middle or final body-paragraph. The littest essays use colorful language to keep their readers engaged. Writers don't want their readers to fall asleep!

Moving on to other points, the middle section is a bit like the meat and potatoes of a delicious dinner. The introduction is a tasty appetizer to get things started, the conclusion is a dainty dessert to finish off the meal, but the middle is where the reader (or eater) gets their fill of knowledge (or food), the main course. The best essays use this space to deliver the facts, research, and substance of their topic. This is where the writer should work to prove their thesis statement.

Hopefully, most essays will be about something a bit more interesting than essays themselves. In that case, the writer should give the reader a treat by giving further information and detail than the required three measly body-paragraphs with three meager sentences. Picking interesting topics and diving into material can often lead to the finest work by the essay writer. Strong argumentative essays, for example, will tackle counterarguments by acknowledging them and responding within the body-paragraphs.

One more thing: well-written essays should use structure effectively by starting new paragraphs for new ideas. Inexperienced writers may take the "three body-paragraph" rule to heart by simply writing three paragraphs, but they would be better served writing a fourth (fifth, sixth...) paragraph for a new idea than to include new information within the last paragraph just for the sake of writing only three body-paragraphs.

When high school teachers, college administrators, and professors read essays, they like to enjoy a solid three course meal. The ticket to a polished, complete essay is to write an introductory paragraph with a strong thesis statement, at least three body-paragraphs, which often include at least three sentences apiece, consisting of different ideas, arguments, analysis, and counterarguments, and a conclusion to wrap everything up. Bon appetit!

This unit obviously covers a ton of stuff. Reading the essays lets me know which points landed and which didn't. I find that generally a healthy skepticism of corporate media is developed and that the essays are hopefully properly formatted and well-written (again, I have a heavy emphasis on working with syntax before big assignments are due). A problem I have encountered when reading this crop of essays is, as I briefly mentioned, that the healthy skepticism can turn into students thinking that corporate media is "fake news." This is an issue that even Chomsky himself has become concerned about with his work being misunderstood or wielded for nefarious purposes. I remind them that in the *Al Jazeera* interview, Chomsky himself says that the *New York Times*, despite its flaws, is still a fantastic comprehensive daily newspaper to read to get a handle on what's going on in the world. The point, of course, is to consume that news through a trained and skeptical eye.

Chapter Six

April/May – Critical Thinking, Conspiracy Theories, and Conspiracies

Right-wing rhetoric has gained serious momentum for years. From Rush Limbaugh in the 80s to Fox News in the 90s to faux-intellects like Ben Shapiro, Jordan Peterson, and the rest of the "Intellectual Dark Web" in recent years, right-wing ideology is everywhere. It's well-produced, polished, and extremely accessible. If we don't dare to discuss political ideology, current events, and an accurate version of history in schools, providing young citizens with the tools to meet certain ill-informed and ahistoric talking points head on, the influence of these self-interested sources will continue to take hold and steer this country in an ignorant direction. These entities indoctrinate viewers into believing in winner-take-all economics, a distorted and incomplete version of US history, ruthless individualism, and a worldview that objectively does not in any way align with the interests of the vast majority of people. Even though they pretend to be bastions of logic and reason, their messaging relies upon ignorance and half-baked truths to survive.

I first stumbled into learning about logic, fallacies, and reason when I read the book *You're Not So Smart* by David McRaney, and I then wished I had learned about such concepts long before. Knowing about cognitive biases and fallacies literally felt like a superpower, a way to clear my own thinking not only in political discussions but in personal relationships as well. Critical thinking is absolutely vital and deserves far more attention in high school classrooms, but I devote a few weeks to it in my journalism class, eventually as a means of debunking conspiracy theories and illogical arguments.

Shapiro has done an interesting thing where he has sort of

held captive the concepts of logic and reason even though he himself is the king of fallacies. For this reason, as Ben Burgis describes at the beginning of his book *Give Them An Argument: Logic for the Left*, many left-leaning people have shied away from studying logic because Shapiro has given the concept itself a sort of putrid connotation with his whole "facts don't care about your feelings" attitude. A classic example of Shapiro's pitiful argumentation is when he went on BBC and was interviewed by Andrew Neil. Neil grilled him on his draconian beliefs regarding abortion, to which Shapiro accused staunchly-conservative Neil of being a "leftist," committing a blend of the strawman and ad-hominem fallacy (he attacked Neil's character instead of what he was saying – a made-up version of his character at that) with zero sense of irony. Even if Neil was a "leftist" or a "Marxist," pointing that out alone does not win an argument, or even make a point. (Hot tip: If a right winger ever disparagingly calls you a "leftist," a "socialist," or a "Marxist," simply ask them what it even means. They have no idea because their only impression of these words and ideas is the disingenuous caricature that right-wing corporate lackeys provided for them.)

Shapiro is touted by media as a wonderkid of logic and reason, the "Cool Kid's Philosopher" (a nickname given in the pages of the "left" *NY Times* for God's sake – they also coined "Intellectual Dark Web"), and yet he blatantly commits a litany of fallacies often when he speaks, but especially this particular instance when he went on this program so grossly unprepared. He was so unprepared, in fact, that his dismal performance can actually provide some wonderful lessons in logic and reason for the classroom. (Side note: to Andrew Neil's credit, he actually held his guest to account and asked the tough questions instead of lob softball questions at him as a means of promoting a book or something. Quite refreshing after observing American corporate media in the previous unit.)

Shapiro commits the tu quoque fallacy (avoiding having

to engage with criticism by turning it back on the accuser – answering criticism with criticism) when Neil questions him on prior statements. Shapiro doesn't have the guts to reckon with what he said, so he just starts accusing the conservative Neil of being a leftist because, well, that's all a guy like Shapiro has when he's not in a discussion with his usual opponents such as young college students. Returning criticism with criticism isn't a real argument – it is blatantly fallacious.

Neil later asks Shapiro about his authoritarian response to abortion – Shapiro agreed 10 years in prison for a woman crossing state lines to get an abortion is acceptable, just as one example. Committing the appeal to authority fallacy (saying that because an authority thinks something, it must therefore be true) he answers "science" as his rationale, even though "science" alone cannot answer the question of when personhood begins, let alone justify the morality, or lack thereof, regarding such extreme policy as a punishment for abortion. You can, of course, support those policies if you like, but it's the furthest thing from "logic and reason" to simply cite "science" as your rationale.

When Shapiro assumes that Neil is not only pro-choice but a "leftist" just because he doesn't agree with his specific draconian measures, he commits the black or white fallacy (where two alternative states are presented as the only possibilities, when in fact more possibilities exist) – you can be pro-life without agreeing with Shapiro's authoritarian stance. There is a lot of gray area here – some pro-life people would like to punish the doctor who performs the abortion, some would not want such harsh sentencing, some wouldn't want any sentencing at all, some would even want to improve material conditions for people and thereby make abortions increasingly rare, etc.

And finally, Shapiro outright lies when he claims he did not put videos up that said he "DESTROYS" people – he had uploaded them before and after this interview occurred on his own page and his publication the *Daily Wire*. Rather than refer to this as a specific fallacy we can just call it exactly what it is: lying.

In Shapiro's defense, he admitted he got owned in this interview, and added it to the list of "dumb things I've said" on his website, which essentially actually means "dumb framings of the beliefs I will never change." However, it's always tempting to really hammer Shapiro since he has built a brand on supposedly using "reason and logic" and "facts don't care about your feelings" (by debating with college kids who are still figuring everything out no less) as he was the fallacy king in this interview and regularly engages in circular logic on his videos. This absolute joke of a commentator is somehow seen as the bastion brain genius in right-wing circles and a beacon of logic and reason. Perhaps on his best day he could do a bit better, but on his worst he is actually a great example of how not to commit fallacies. Ironically, Ben Shapiro truly is a great teacher when it comes to logic and reason because either his imagination or his honesty regarding the issues is so utterly limited he feels he must resort to completely fallacious argumentation. Showing high school students an example of this type of intellectual theater they may encounter online is a worthwhile exercise.

Truly studying critical thinking is an incredibly enlightening experience. It lifts these clouds in your mind. It relieves that nagging feeling of encountering an argument you just know makes absolutely zero sense but you can't quite put your finger on why that is the case – giving logically incoherent arguments a name really helps to identify them in yourself and others. As I always mention, even though parents often have every right and every reason to say, "because I said so!" this command is not necessarily built on a logical premise. We would need further information to make that decision.

The bumbling escapades of Ben Shapiro aren't the only resource for this. As I mentioned, Ben Burgis has a wonderful book on the subject (which, almost as a prerequisite, takes Shapiro to task throughout). But after initial introductions on these concepts (there's many great videos on YouTube), two absolutely wonderful resources are yourbias.is and yourlogicalfallacyis.com.

Each site introduces the purpose up front: "Cognitive biases make our judgments irrational. We have evolved to use shortcuts in our thinking, which are often useful, but a cognitive bias means there's a kind of misfiring going on causing us to lose objectivity. This website has been designed to help you identify some of the most common biases stuffing up your thinking."

And the fallacy site: "A logical fallacy is a flaw in reasoning. Logical fallacies are like tricks or illusions of thought, and they're often very sneakily used by politicians and the media to fool people. Don't be fooled! This website has been designed to help you identify and call out dodgy logic wherever it may raise its ugly, incoherent head."

Each website features 24 examples of biases and fallacies apiece. I take the time to go through every single one with the students and come up with additional examples which often relate to current events to keep it relevant.

We've already examined a few fallacies with the Shapiro debacle, but let's look at a few more using the COVID-19 mask fiasco of 2020. When right-wing commenters claimed, "first it's masks, the next thing you know you'll be forced to wear a burka (or some other absurd claim)," that is an example of the slippery slope fallacy: "You said that if we allow A to happen, then Z will eventually happen too, therefore A should not happen."

When we see people saying, "why should we care about COVID-19 (or some other issue) when child trafficking is going on?" that is an example of the appeal to emotion fallacy: "You attempted to manipulate an emotional response in place of a valid or compelling argument." Of course child trafficking is a problem, but that doesn't mean that COVID-19 isn't also a problem, but there is an obvious emotional appeal when child-victims become the talking-point. If you point this out to someone and they say, "oh so I guess you're saying you don't care about human trafficking then?" that is an example of a strawman fallacy: "You misrepresented someone's argument to make it easier to attack." And, of course, when Uncle QAnon says, "And you better believe Wayfair is involved because they named expensive furniture after missing children and are now selling kids right on their website!" they have committed the false cause fallacy (quite prevalent among conspiracy theory circles): "You presumed that a real or perceived relationship between things means that one is the cause of the other."

And then we shift from logic in arguments to cognitive biases. There are all sorts of examples that seem to be everywhere today – confirmation bias: You favor things that confirm your existing beliefs – think back to users on social media believing what they want to believe before even investigating the truth. Backfire bias: When some aspect of your core beliefs is challenged, it can cause you to believe even more strongly – think about that friend or family member who you've tried to convince to hear you out and confronting them with facts just makes them mad and drives them further away. The framing effect: you allow yourself to be unduly influenced by context and delivery – think back to George Lakoff's points on framing, or Neil Cavuto's disingenuous framing in his interviews with the young women in favor of taxpayer-funded higher education. The just-world hypothesis: Your preference for justice makes you presume it exists – just because you believe in law and order and things went well for you doesn't mean that other people haven't gotten a raw deal. These are biases that linger in all humans. Not knowing about them makes them difficult to keep in check.

When we analyze the wonderful examples the site provides and come up with our own examples as teachers and as a class, we begin to see that fallacies and biases worm their way into all sorts of scenarios. A wonderful homework assignment is to have the kids be on the lookout for a bias and fallacy over the course of a weekend – one of each committed by someone else, and one of each committed by themselves.

I would say the most critical thing to point out when teaching this stuff is that it is very easy to take this basic understanding of fallacies and biases and use it to own people in arguments – but most importantly students should be aware that biases and fallacies exist in every single person – including themselves. If you are aware that these things exist not only in others but yourself as well, the better chance you have of making sure you avoid falling victim to them. Of course, at one point or another everyone has the potential to fall victim to biases and commit fallacies trying to justify ourselves, but if you know something about yourself, it seems obvious you are less likely to repeatedly make the same mistakes again and again. Furthermore, if you understand that you are as susceptible to this stuff as any other person, you gain a sense of humility about humans as imperfect beings and could be a little more understanding of people committing fallacies and falling victim to cognitive biases when you encounter them. As the curse of knowledge bias says on yourbias.is: "Once you understand something you presume it to be obvious to everyone. Things make sense once they make sense, so it can be hard to remember why they didn't. We build complex networks of understanding and forget how intricate the path to our available knowledge really is."

It goes on to give the advice, "When teaching someone something new, go slow and explain like they're 10 years old (without being patronizing). Repeat key points and facilitate active practice to help embed knowledge."

As I tell my kids, I am not an expert of logic and reason. What I am giving them is an introduction on this stuff, things to be aware of, not only when analyzing conspiracy theories or political arguments, but most importantly when conducting oneself in relationships and arguments every single day. This is definitely one of those things I badly wish was taught to me at a younger age, and I can now only try to offer that to other people. Keep it engaging for students, think not only of examples that apply to current events but also examples they can really relate to as kids: when parents appeal to emotion when they say, "eat your veggies, there are starving kids in third world countries" or when gossip turns into ad-hominem attacks on a person. Fellow high school teachers reading this may not be experts on this stuff but they are very capable of reading up on this themselves and passing it along.

Applying media literacy and critical thinking to disinformation

There are millions of people, including members of congress, who think that a Trump-appointed secret investigator named Q is doing inside work to expose the deep state and uncover the truth about Satanic cannibalistic pedophiles running Hollywood, the Democratic Party, and the government in general...or something like that (as we found out in the HBO docuseries *Q: Into the Storm*, "Q" is possibly former 8chan administrator Ron Watkins making things up to keep gullible people on his website).

Like any good story there's a kernel of truth. Director Wes Craven was commenting on sexual abuse in Hollywood back in 2000 when he released *Scream 3* – interestingly enough a movie produced by the disgraced sexual assailant producer Harvey Weinstein. The Clintons, Donald Trump, and other powerful people have ties to the pedophile Jefferey Epstein, who was never able to speak, as it seems like the most powerful are never held to account and never face the music for their dirty deeds. When this begins to make less and less sense for people, without a level-headed, rational critique of the insane power dynamics and structures in this country, intricate stories that produce simplistic answers emerge to make sense of the madness while heroes are made of undeserving characters such as Trump. All the while, the right wing enjoys the fact that the blame for this country's failures is so displaced and the reality of the situation is so bastardized.

Perhaps I am naive and the forces of the internet would always result in conspiracy theories gaining stunning momentum that force the madness to the mainstream, but I'd like to think if media literacy, critical thinking, and an honest look at the flaws of this country were taught in class, such lunacy wouldn't blossom in the way it has here in America.

For a moment I'd like to discuss my own brush with conspiracy theories. When I was about 25, I had been living an experience similar to many other millennials. I graduated from college in 2009 at the height of the Great Recession. I moved home with my parents and struggled to find a job until I found one making $11 an hour working as a reporter for a local weekly newspaper. I was laid off once, used my college degree painting houses for a while, and was eventually hired back a few months later after the other reporter at my old paper retired. About a year later the paper closed for good and I was unemployed. I liked being a reporter, but desperate for a job I switched gears and started work at a behavioral health school making about $13 an hour as an Ed Tech III. For any readers who haven't had a stint working in behavioral health before, this is a brutal job working with kids who are saddled with the heartbreaking stew of trauma, intellectual disabilities, behavioral issues, poverty, etc. and when they get upset you can find yourself punched, kicked, spat on, and verbally lambasted multiple times a day every single day for as long as you work the job.

It's a very necessary job, as America can't seem to break the chains of poverty and trauma causing generations of families to suffer from poor living conditions, but the pay sucked, the administration was severely out of touch, and it was mentally and physically exhausting. Comradery among staff was essentially the only benefit other than knowing you were at least trying to better humanity, no matter how thankless, slow-moving, and impossible it often felt on the job.

If you come from a decent background, you don't really realize the clients you work with at a school like this even exist. When you look around at the lavish world that celebrities and politicians live in, the high life depicted constantly on American media, it becomes difficult to wrap your mind around why on earth someone should be worth billions of dollars while entire schools-worth of kids with severe trauma and disabilities around the country live in households that can't even afford to put food on the table or a heating bill in the dead of winter. When you take a step out of your insular bubble you begin to see that there is a lot deeply wrong with the country, with the world we live in. When you pair this reality with the rhetoric of "personal responsibility," that poor people deserve what they get, that they had it coming and just didn't work hard enough (the children who have never even had an opportunity to go to work within these families be damned, I guess) you start to look for answers as to why the hell things are the way they are. I believe when people are told the right-wing story that poor people deserve to live in squalor because they didn't work hard enough, the rich must have worked incredibly hard to amass their fortune, and the magic of the free market somehow produces a just and rational world, people become cynical about the way everything supposedly works.

Around this time I sought to figure out why the world worked the way it did. I had always had an interest in politics, but more as a partisan fanboy of the Democratic Party, not as a deep thinker about economic and power systems and things like that. Who was in control? Who pulled the strings in the world?

Like the hypothetical student I mentioned previously in this chapter stumbling across a *Prager U* or Ben Shapiro video, I stumbled into *Loose Change: An American Coup* on Netflix at some point in this quest. The widely debunked and misleading film, which we will look at in depth shortly, is a documentary that asks a bunch of hanging open-ended questions and ultimately urges the viewer to consider that perhaps the Bush/Cheney administration somehow directly destroyed the buildings on 9/11 with controlled demolitions and missiles. I knew going in I hated the Bush administration and also felt the same as many Americans, that things are increasingly off-the-rails in this country and the world in general.

While I obviously escaped the quicksand of conspiracy theories (if even one conspiracy theory gets you, the rest start to seem incredibly plausible as well, and your internet algorithms these days make sure you see the lot of them) I admit I was intrigued. I made a since-deleted Facebook post about how 9/11 was potentially an "inside job." I thought it just might be possible that Bush/Cheney orchestrated the attack as a way to go into Iraq and make a bunch of money. I felt empowered that I knew something that a lot of other people hadn't taken the time to know about.

But that thing I had done was watch a 90-minute documentary made by a couple of amateur filmmakers cobbling together a half-baked and easily-debunked narrative. Not exactly extensive research. Not exactly the cross-referencing and critical eye I teach students today. I thought I had some elevated sense of what happened that tragic day because I took a mere 90 minutes to watch an extremely one-sided, terribly researched documentary with a predetermined conclusion baked in and a bunch of hanging questions that the filmmakers chose not to answer even though they could have.

But I was at least curious to learn more. I remember there was another 9/11 documentary on Netflix at the time. I am not certain because I can't find it now, but I believe it was a documentary based on the *Popular Mechanics* journalism on this very topic (I use the book *Debunking 9/11 Myths: Why Conspiracy Theories Can't Stand Up to the Facts* in class).

The documentary confronted the purveyors of the *Loose Change* conspiracy theory with hard-hitting experiments and evidence that put into serious jeopardy their original theories, which is exactly why so many different iterations of *Loose Change* exist – they had to keep moving the goalposts (the special pleading fallacy – making up exceptions and reinventing claims when a claim is shown to be false) to keep their theory intact. The same documentary also revealed a very simple point that, for me, said a lot: imagine how many people would have to be involved keeping the controlled demolition of two of the largest buildings in the entire world a secret. A handful of people in a back room can't just roll out tons of dynamite in secret. The family members of the people who died on those planes, which *Loose Change* and other similar theories claim didn't exist, wouldn't just keep quiet if their loved ones were whisked away and eliminated by some government agency. When you begin to think of the logistics of such a theory rather than fall victim to the framing effect and take such a documentary at face value, the entire thing falls apart.

But more on *Loose Change* later. As I began to read more and look at legitimate sources that explained the way the world worked (for me *Power Systems* by Noam Chomsky was a real eye-opener) I started to realize there are plenty of issues to point the finger at without subscribing to some absurd theory about controlled demolition and talcum powder. America invaded Iraq even though Iraq had nothing to do with the 9/11 attacks. There were conflicts of interest with Dick Cheney's Haliburton making millions off of the war. 9/11 resulted in various civil liberties being eroded, in particular warrantless spying on US citizens. The CIA started torturing people, many of whom were innocent (not that torture is ever acceptable, or even beneficial from an intelligence standpoint, in a civilized world). The issues surrounding 9/11 don't need some crazy story to be interesting or to draw connections as to how it has impacted our lives, the conventional story is horrifying enough.

And, of course, as Ana Merlan points out in her book *Republic of Lies: American Conspiracy Theorists and Their Surprising Rise to Power*, there is a huge difference between conspiracies and conspiracy theories. The CIA really did perform experiments on human subjects with its MK-Ultra program. The FBI and law enforcement really did surveil, harass, and assassinate black leaders with its COINTELPRO program. The CIA really did torture people, and after reading Tom O'Neil's *CHAOS* I have questions about the Manson murders as well. This is the government of "the greatest country on earth" demonstrably doing overtly nefarious deeds. In the private sector you have entities that actively make money off of destructive war (such as Cheney's Haliburton) and a media class that sold the war to the public. While America's Democrats fetishize the intelligence, Republicans look for "deep state" influence in all the wrong places.

I've had many discussions over the years with people who believed in fairytale stories such as COVID-19 conspiracy theories, the supposed "fraud" in the 2020 election, or others who fell for the Sandy Hook conspiracy theory which claimed all of the people involved in the tragic shooting of an elementary school were just actors trying to push gun control legislation. A common line from the savvier members in this crowd is, "hey look at how the media did us after 9/11, getting us into the Iraq War" or "you think a government capable of MK-Ultra couldn't do Sandy Hook?" Analyzing the differences in these conspiracies vs. conspiracy theories, which boil down to wonderful journalists uncovering facts, evidence, and the reality of the situation instead of drawing loose connections with a predetermined theory in mind from the onset, is an incredibly important defense against the inevitable next-conspiracy-theory in our online world where ideas spread in the blink of an eye.

Before going down these more involved paths I recommend showing some introductory videos of how conspiracy theories work, why they can be enticing, and how to resist them by noticing they constantly change and grow larger so as to endlessly support the predetermined conclusion.

You can also start, or even just use, some lighter examples if you don't want to get too political. Three I use briefly in the introduction to the larger unit on 9/11 and *Loose Change* are the moon landing, flat earth theory, and crop circles.

There are endless resources in debunking the absurdities of flat earth theory and the moon landing online. Crop circles is an example I use early on in the unit because it's a bit more personal for me.

Around the time I was flirting with 9/11 conspiracy theories, a co-worker told me I just had to watch this documentary *Thrive*, which essentially claims aliens are trying to tell us about how to organize a utopia but the message is suppressed by the government. There's a portion of the documentary that heavily uses the framing effect to show lavish crop circle creations that are so intricate they *must* be made from beings that are literally out of this world. To make this point, it shows a handful of badly-human-made crop circles as "proof" that human beings could never pull off such a feat (which could be considered the negativity bias – allowing a poor example of something to influence your thinking).

I show students the *Thrive* clip (right on YouTube) which discusses these crop circles. We have a discussion about the plausibility of aliens and the idea that the clip serves as proof that the crop circles are indeed made by extraterrestrials. We discuss whether or not it's possible for people to make an intricate crop circle. Answers vary across the board.

Then I show them a clip on YouTube titled *Unmasked – Secrets of Deception – Crop Circles*. The clip follows a team of three guys who are able to make an extremely intricate crop circle, which they had drawn up earlier that day, in the middle of the night, silently, undetected, in a matter of hours.

It's important to note this also doesn't inherently mean that aliens haven't visited us, and certainly doesn't mean they're not real at all. It simply means the crop circles as framed on documentaries and content like *Thrive* are using half-baked evidence to support their predetermined conclusion that aliens are among us, trying to communicate with us and the government overlords aren't allowing it to happen. Human beings are capable of doing intricate crop circles which is very problematic to the idea that they're made by aliens. Furthermore, I find using the online clips is helpful because, let's be honest, they're teenagers and that's where they're getting information. I do my best to urge them to read information from more thorough and substantial sources, but making some sense out of the vastness of the internet seems like a worthwhile goal as well. The main point to be made is providing the evidence that connects crop circles to alien life.

Anyway, this is generally the theme of conspiracy theories. If I didn't know any better, I'd wonder if intelligentsia or private sector special interests were covertly putting this information out as a way of completely discrediting the government and massaging public opinion into believing we'd be better off with decisions, wealth, and resources in the hands of a small, unelected, and unaccountable private sector, but I don't want to get too conspiratorial.

I have even found through the years the alarming reality that a lot of students seem to use the concept of "government" as essentially synonymous with nefarious behavior and corruption itself. For example, when we discuss how corporate media is able to manipulate public opinion, and Facebook and Google can spy on people to a certain degree, a general comment often muttered by students will be something to the effect of, *man the government sure is screwed up.*

While they're correct in many ways, we shouldn't allow things like the government and taxes as concepts that are neither inherently good or evil to be demonized like that. I like pointing out to my kids that my salary is paid for by taxes. The roads that got them to school are paid for by taxes. The supplies we have at school are paid for by taxes, and the lack of supplies, programs, or classes is due to a lack of tax revenue. Additionally, we vote for politicians who decide to spend our tax dollars. Elected people within a government may misbehave and advocate for policies that harm the masses, but the government as a concept, as well as our tax dollars, is what we make of it. Reinforcing this indisputable reality often I believe could go a long way in helping kids take a step back and critically think about right-wing talking points. Conspiracy theories have a way of completely eroding trust in the government across the board, laying the groundwork for privatization to make its case, when in reality we should take a far more nuanced look.

Eventually we move on to thoroughly investigating *Loose Change: An American Coup*. The movie begins by referencing a bunch of questionable activities that governments have engaged in, with some blatantly inaccurate historical accounts mixed in as well. For example, the movie mentions that Franklin Roosevelt knew that Pearl Harbor was coming (he didn't) and also later mentions that bankers tried to overthrow FDR (they indeed tried). This sort of conflation with historical realities and made-up nonsense is a way conspiracy theories thrive, but it's also worth pointing out that as this sort of shady activity continues to go on and the perpetrators continue to get away with it, it causes citizens, with good reason I would say, to grow increasingly distrustful of elected governments.

As mentioned, the Popular Mechanics book *Debunking 9/11 Myths* is a great source in refuting the miserable *Loose Change* story, which its creator, Dylan Avery, has since backed away from. The story, in short, makes a bunch of loose suggestions: perhaps the hijackers weren't really who the media said they were, which would mean the media was not only complicit in the entire coup, but also declined making a boatload of money by neglecting to break the story of the century that 9/11 was an "inside job." The movie also claims perhaps a plane didn't really hit the Pentagon despite countless eyewitness reports and wreckage found on site, not to mention the fact that if Flight 77 wasn't really hijacked and it was instead, as insinuated, a missile, that would mean everyone on that flight either just went home that night or was destroyed secretly by some sort of secret government force.

Other inferences or claims made: the buildings actually underwent a controlled demolition because a plane couldn't really bring down a building even though countless structural engineers and high-rise building experts have stated otherwise. The film actually gets their own "expert" (in an unrelated field: see appeal to authority fallacy) in Doug Jones, who, like the quack from the internet classic *Plandemic*, goes against the expert-consensus and goes rogue. People assume they must be right because they like to have their confirmation bias tickled and because trust in institutions is increasingly sliding.

I recommend watching the entire *Loose Change* film and pausing it frequently to debunk what is being said. It's far enough removed from political dialog that it's not super controversial, but it is a wonderful illustration as to how this sort of content works: frame it through the lens of the predetermined conclusion, ignore all opposing evidence to the contrary, draw incredibly loose connections, keep the viewer wondering by asking questions, etc. *Loose Change* provides ample opportunity to do this with a group of kids in a safe and controlled environment. Drawing connections to other absurd conspiracy theories will help students understand they might be viewing misleading and incomplete information when they inevitably encounter it thereafter. I believe it is much more effective to give students and future citizens these tools than to depend on the masters of gigantic tech platforms to do fact-checking for us.

A fantastic supplement to both the documentary and the *Popular Mechanics* book is a debate with both the *Loose Change* film makers, Dylan Avery and Jason Bermas, and both authors of *Debunking*, James Meigs and David Dunbar, on *Democracy Now!* with Amy Goodman. Goodman does a fantastic job of being objective in the interview and the responses speak for themselves. Avery, who actually at times in the debate noticeably shows signs of a young man who doesn't quite fully believe what he's gotten himself into, and especially Bermas, grow increasingly frustrated when confronted with hard evidence and coherent explanations in response to the loose questions they posed in various versions of their documentary. The clips from *Loose Change* played in the *Democracy Now!* interview are actually different than the version I show in class because it's actually an earlier version of the film – they had to move the goalposts to make sure the theory remained intact. The debate is truly a treasure for this unit because it is a rare moment when conspiracy theorists are confronted unabashedly by real journalists with another fantastic journalist mediating the situation.

There are countless points for this unit I still haven't made here, and I won't take up too much space going into many more, but there is also the case of Barry Jennings from *Loose Change*. Jennings was in Building 7, which eventually collapsed after burning unattended all day, and gave an interview for *Loose Change* about how he heard "explosions."

Putting aside the fact that he's the only eyewitness interviewed (since he told filmmakers what they wanted to hear), Jennings himself later told the BBC he didn't like how he was portrayed in the film. Versions of the film that came out after Jennings went on record saying *he didn't like how he was portrayed* claimed that he "died unexpectedly," and that a private investigator wanted nothing to do with the case, leaving the viewer to believe Jennings was potentially offed by some servant of the lizard overlords who wanted to stifle the truth.

In reality, Jennings came down with leukemia out of nowhere and it killed him very quickly. His family was harassed by conspiracy theorists because the grifters who put this disinformation out there have people who never took a media literacy class eating out of the palms of their hands. This is quite reminiscent of the heartbreaking travesty that went on with the families of Sandy Hook victims when scumbags like Alex Jones were claiming that the shooting was a false flag operation to try to take guns. Sure, it might be my own appeal to emotion, but if the overarching societal damage dealt by these sorts of conspiracies doesn't hit home, the fact that these suffering families have to also deal with cranks harassing them can pull at the heart strings from a different direction.

The assignment for this unit is simple: students must debunk a conspiracy theory using their knowledge of logical fallacies/ cognitive biases, along with their ability to find credible research and legitimate sources of information. I ask them to include the following:

§ At least three reputable resources used to help learn enough to debunk the chosen conspiracy theory. These will come from credible news outlets, journalists, researchers, and, with its flaws, corporate media.

§ Identify three cognitive biases/logical fallacies the conspiracy theorists commit in their claim – do this by stating the argument made by the conspiracy theorist and effectively argue against their position using facts and evidence.

I allow students to debunk their conspiracy theory using an essay or a slideshow and provide them with a list of ideas to debunk (I have mentioned many here already, but there's also "PizzaGate," the theory Hillary Clinton was running a pedophile ring in the basement of a pizza parlor, the "faked moon landing," and more).

* * *

As the students work on their final journalism assignment of the year, we go in depth regarding what happened in the aftermath of 9/11. Like anyone else around my age, we remember exactly where we were (English class for me) when the towers hit and the TVs were wheeled into classrooms to watch the story live.

I must note, before we even watch *Loose Change* I show the class the raw footage of 9/11 from the film *102 Minutes That Changed America*. It's easy to forget that these kids weren't even born when this life-altering thing happened. Some kids who thought they had a handle on what happened that day approach me afterwards and mention they didn't realize the buildings collapsed, didn't realize multiple buildings were hit, and other understandable misconceptions. Of course this stuff is hard to watch, but again, it was nearly 20 years ago at this point. Doing a unit on this recent historical moment and providing context as to what happened thereafter, I believe is a fantastic exercise for preparing students for future shocks, such as COVID-19, in an educational environment.

When I first watched *Loose Change*, I hated the Bush administration and knew our government was fucked up, so it confirmed my bias in all the worst ways. A bunch of people I worked with at the time had similar feelings and we further confirmed each other's biases by discussing it and validating each other. When I started to read more and seek answers, I found that no credible journalists were on board with this or any of the other crazy conspiracy theories. The people peddling these sorts of theories were content creators like Avery and Bermas, not serious investigative journalists like Naomi Klein,

Amy Goodman, or Jeremy Scahill, or serious thinkers like Noam Chomsky or Cornel West. If these people weren't talking about this massive story, is it because they were also in on it? Or is it more plausible there was no evidence in the first place?

The sort of things these thinkers and journalists were talking about as a result of 9/11 were abundant – and in many ways equally horrifying. America entered wars that ultimately killed hundreds of thousands of civilians, some of which were doing things as unrelated to terrorism as attending a wedding. America started torturing people. America increased the military budget to the delight of Vice President Dick Cheney's former company Haliburton, which not only gave him a fat payout before joining the presidential ticket but made tons of money as a company because of the war. America spends trillions on this so-called "War on Terror" while 30,000 people die per year due to lack of healthcare (while a great many also go into debt) and hundreds of thousands live homeless. Domestically, we've seen civil liberties eroded in the form of warrantless government spying on US citizens.

As journalism by Chomsky, Scahill, Klein, and many more outline, those hundreds of thousands of innocent Middle Eastern civilians died as US corporations tried to capitalize on the destabilized region. And as Major Danny Sjursen points out in a wonderful *The Nation Magazine* article titled *What if This Had Happened on the Day After 9/11?* a smarter move would have been to exercise restraint after the dreaded attack rather than pretend we had to go blow up the place because "they hate our freedom."

Sjursen points out in the article that though the attack on 9/11 was obviously horrific, it wasn't because they desperately "hated our freedom" (whatever the hell that even means):

WHY THEY (REALLY) HATED US
Americans and their government were inclined to accept the

most simplistic explanation for the terror attacks of 9/11. As George W. Bush would assure us all, Osama bin Laden and Al Qaeda just "hate us for our freedoms." The end.

Something about the guilelessness of that explanation, which was the commonplace one of that moment, never quite seemed right. Human motivations and actions are almost always more complex, more multifaceted, less simpleminded than that. While Bush boiled it all down to "Islamic" fundamentalism, even a cursory look at bin Laden's written declaration of "war" – or as he called it, jihad – demonstrates that his actual focus was far more secular and less explicitly religious than was suggested at the time. Couched between Koranic verses, bin Laden listed three all-too-worldly grievances with America:

§ The US military had occupied bases in the vicinity of Saudi Arabia's holy sites of Mecca and Medina. (Well...that had indeed been the case, at least since 1990, if not earlier.)

§ US-imposed sanctions on Iraq had caused the deaths of hundreds of thousands of Iraqi children. (This was, in fact, a reality that even Secretary of State Madeleine Albright awkwardly acknowledged.)

§ America's leaders had long favored Israeli interests to the detriment of Palestinian well-being or national aspirations. (A bit simplistic, but true enough. One could, in fact, stock several bookshelves with respected works substantiating bin Laden's claim on this point.)

To state the obvious, none of this faintly justified the mass murder of civilians in New York and Washington. Nonetheless, at that moment, an honest analysis of an adversary's motives would have been prudent.

The media definitely helped sell the War on Terror and the claim that the attack itself had something to do with "hating our freedom" instead of honestly reporting the actual grievances as

Sjursen did. In the case of the Iraq War, there is literally not a humane explanation for destroying the country. Sjursen's points provide substantial and legitimate critiques of power instead of sending us on a wild goose chase about controlled demolitions and conspiracies. The insane story told by a documentary like *Loose Change* rightly suspects trouble is afoot but completely misses the mark in offering a sensible critique of power. Just as I witnessed countless people wonder if COVID-19 might be the start of Agenda 21 ("they" are going to depopulate the world by 90 percent using vaccines or something) as Congress voted to hand over an ungodly transfer of wealth to the already-wealthy while working people got $1200 and a housing crisis, a good many people were looking in the wrong place for shady activity while the heist went on right in front of their faces, as reported on openly by the distrusted media.

The Right accuses this sort of honesty, viewing objective reality as somehow bad because it doesn't paint America in a heroic, infallible light. How the hell are things ever to improve if we can't look at ourselves honestly and think about how we might be better? What kind of an attitude is that? I believe teaching what I have written about here is imperative in creating a better world and should be taught in schools across the country. I also know that it's possible some of my moral conclusions within these pages might be off. I know that each year I will get better at teaching it, I know each year I will hone my delivery and find even better sources to use in class. That's striving for success. The idea that we should be painting this country as an infallible source of goodness is frankly the opposite of everything this country supposedly represents, it's the opposite of patriotism. Politicians should be held to the fire, voters should be aware of the failings of a country so they can organize and participate in democracy accordingly, workers should be aware of their power as laborers, and viewing really any entity or person as infallible is a huge mistake. If we don't take an honest, hard look at what we have done around the world, and the brutal history of our country itself, particularly to people of color and immigrants, we are not only destined to continue that behavior, but I would argue get worse over time.

The way things are right now is not set in stone. We can imagine and demand a better world, a better country. Even if the argument is true that America is the best country, and we should be grateful for iPhones and Starbucks (as hacks like Shapiro, Prager, and Peterson like to argue) we should still strive for being an even better country than as we exist now. The reality is this country is imperfect, as any country is, but shielding those imperfections isn't patriotic, it's Status Quo Warrioring that has no place in progressivism on behalf of the greater good. Realizing the country is flawed but chasing the rabbit of conspiracy theories instead of taking the time to learn the truth is no better.

Conclusion

As the debate surrounding returning to school mid-pandemic in the summer of 2020 raged on, Fox News's Laura Ingraham had guest Rebecca Freidrichs (who later spoke at the Republican National Convention that summer) on to make the following statement:

> The unions are using the closure of our schools as a smokescreen. Here's why: sadly these unions are actually using our schools to sexualize our children and to train them in anti-American ideology. They do this with a coalition of over 180 organizations including sadly the CDC, Planned Parenthood, and Black Lives Matter Inc. It is shocking what they are teaching our children online through virtual learning. They're teaching our children to sext, to view pornography, they are hooking them up with online sex experts, so what they are doing is grooming our children for sexual predators to use them. This is child abuse. I have an editorial about this tomorrow online in the Washington Times, people can read and learn all the details. This is one of the reasons unions want to keep our schools closed because they can sneak these evil lessons past loving teachers who have no idea by keeping them virtual.

If that's not completely insane enough, her piece was indeed printed in the *Washington Times* under the headline *How public schools groom kids for sexual predators like Epstein and Maxwell.*

After complaining about sex education in schools with more loose and unfounded drivel, she gets to the real point and the purpose of making her insane claims at the end of the article:

> This is outrageous. And it's precisely why our Founders

never intended for our schools to be "public" or controlled by government and union forces. It's also why the recent Supreme Court decision permitting religious schools to benefit from private school-choice programs brings hope. Now all we need is to expose the misuse of "separation of church and state" so that all children can be educated free from government intrusion and free from perverts masquerading as experts and educators.

Like any good conservative foot soldier (she's literally featured on the American Legislative Exchange Council website, a far-right organization which aims to endlessly privatize) the goal is to bust unions, erode public institutions, and clearly say anything, no matter how baseless and insane, to achieve these goals. The Right has waged war on the public sector, unions, education, equality, and working people for decades, so the idea that schools should shy away from political matters and discussion of power structures is extremely dangerous, inherently right wing, and ultimately self-destructive. The Right paints moderate right-wing figures such as Joe Biden and Kamala Harris as "socialists," just as Freidrichs paints an innocuous public school system as this insane radicalized institution that breeds victims of pedophilia. This is what a major political party and their media arm is doing while the other has no answers, no agenda, and seemingly very little willingness or ability to do anything about anything.

Donald Trump himself talked about a "patriotic education" toward the end of his presidency, which apparently means to describe America in only the most positive way possible. Anything else would apparently be unacceptable and unAmerican. He went on to say at a September 2020 rally that it means making sure Confederate statues remain standing, since that's apparently the only way to preserve, acknowledge, or understand history, we'd never be able to remember anything otherwise. Trump lamented Robert E. Lee, who if mentioned in a class of mine would be described as a general who fought to preserve the institution of slavery. Although a historical fact, this would be an unacceptable lesson in the eyes of right wingers because preserving a fuzzy feeling about American exceptionalism is, in the minds of far too many, more important than an accurate description of what our country is, was, and is destined to continue to be if we don't start fighting back ideologically.

In other classes, I teach different things I haven't really discussed in this book: the history of race in America from slavery to segregation to Jim Crow to mass incarceration, authoritarian governments, different economic models and philosophies including Marxism, reallocating tax dollars from wars to social programs or from prisons to rehabilitation centers, historical examples of strikes, unions, wielding power as working-class citizens, and a host of other issues that I believe must be discussed in schools around the country. When we read *1984* in my freshman English class, a major theme is pointing out that if the masses of proletariats had access to information, withheld their labor and fought back, life could improve for them. "If there was hope it must lie in the proles," as Winston Smith speculates.

Trump views this sort of critical look at our country literally, as he boldly stated later in September of 2020, as a form of "child abuse" and describes matters like slavery and systemic racism being taught in schools as a, "crusade against American history [that is] toxic propaganda, ideological poison that, if not removed, will dissolve the civic bonds that tie us together. It will destroy our country." When the sitting president of a country considers it "child abuse" when teachers educate, we may need a robust and active mechanism combating such overt authoritarianism and celebration of ignorance. Mindlessly cheering on a country and ignoring its problems is not education. Ignoring existing problems makes it impossible to create a better world.

Here in Maine, a teacher in Bangor was outed in a pro-Trump Facebook group for...teaching. A lesson about racism was shared against school policy in the group causing Trump supporters to share the video hundreds of times. The unnamed teacher said this within her lesson, "The fact that my race is white is part of my privileged identity. Race is not something that gets in the way of me getting a job or puts me in danger, whereas my gender being female is something I have to think about and might be one of my more targeted identities." This triggered the Trump supporters to call it "unbelievable" and even call for the teacher's firing – or as others call it, "canceling." When we look at trends and hard data, sadly black people are indeed disproportionately unemployed, but the goal of the Right is to cancel history and information and install their own warped version of the world through censorship of reality. This is precisely why the seemingly-mundane claim "you can't be political in classrooms" is so dangerous and so completely wrong. Anything these anti-reality people don't like can be deemed "too political" and consequently potentially suffer censorship or cancelation. No intelligent examination is needed; as long as something could possibly be construed under the massive umbrella of "politics" it is grounds for cancelation according to impediments of progress and Status Quo Warriors. If you're not allowed to discuss or know about this stuff, as was the case in Oceania in 1984, ignorance clearly prevails.

Horace Mann, the father of the common (public) school system, said, "Education, then, beyond all other devices of human origin, is the great equalizer of the conditions of men, the balance wheel of the social machinery." Prior to Mann's work, the school system required tuition fees and was obviously not available to the overwhelming majority of US citizens. Making public education a human right is indeed a great equalizer.

Privatizing the school system does not guarantee everyone gets a chance, and the continued erosion of public schools as private schools are bolstered shows the direction right-wing entities want to go. The point of attacking public schools, aside from slamming unions and at the risk of oversimplification, is to make private education entities money, poor kids be damned. Not exactly the equalizer Mann had envisioned.

The private sector only has the capacity to make things happen if there is a consumer base. This is precisely why the private sector is completely incapable of dealing with homelessness, why it was incapable of dealing with COVID-19 (preemptively or months afterwards), or why poor kids would be left behind in an increasingly privatized school system as the public system faces cuts while the fossil fuel industry and other corporations receive subsidies and the ultra-rich receive tax breaks. In Mann's day, teaching kids to read and write was an equalizer; today teaching high school kids how the world actually works and how propaganda is weaponized could serve as a second great equalizer in this country.

Education, like journalism, is a pillar of democracy. When we pretend that political matters should be left out of the classroom, we usher in, as the late great Michael Brooks argues in his wonderful book *Against the Web: A Cosmopolitan Answer to the New Right*, "The Intellectual Dark Web" – figures such as Ben Shapiro, Jordan Peterson, Dave Rubin, or Sam Harris – to provide answers about the way economics, politics, power, and the world in general works using revised history through a corporatized and authoritarian lens. These entities pretend to just call balls and strikes with no particular lean to their positions, but as we analyzed in the unit on bias, complete impartiality is out the window even if by virtue of the fact that omission and emphasis are inherent mechanisms which reveal bias. When we view what these guys are actually saying it's increasingly obvious they're either dullards who don't know as much as they pretend to know amid their intellectual theater or are, perhaps more nefariously, intentionally lying to and manipulating the public. The reason they blatantly mischaracterize what Marxism and leftism actually mean, the reason they create a strawman caricature out of everything they disagree with, is because they cannot in any meaningful way reckon with the actual ideas being presented.

There are also popular cable pundits like Tucker Carlson. In 2020 a judge threw out a defamation lawsuit on the grounds argued by Fox News that "no reasonable person" takes Carlson seriously. Bill O'Reilly and Alex Jones have used similar defenses through the years, arguing they aren't even actually delivering news, but rather (apparently mindless) entertainment instead. Contrary to what these grifters claim, I am a very pro-speech leftist. I don't want these voices silenced, censored, or "canceled." I want there to be fewer unreasonable and ignorant people in the world. If "no reasonable person" would take them seriously, considering their viewerships, we apparently have a lot of unreasonable people. We need to create reasonable generations from here on out. As a high school teacher, I have a significant opportunity to guide thousands of students in my career out of the dark on the issues that matter to them, who will hopefully spread this knowledge on to people they know, and I will be damned if I miss that opportunity. We're at a point where arguing against what I am teaching, as I think I articulated thoroughly in this book, would often be at odds with reality itself. It's time we take reality back by better educating our youth and move forward in a reasonable, humane, and logical direction. It's time we stopped allowing ourselves to be gaslighted by the irrational madness of the powerful elite.

Early in the Joe Biden presidency, conversations about how to "take reality back" hit the press. *The New York Times* floated a number of ideas, including the concept of a "task force" led by a "reality czar." According to the *Times*, the department would be "a centralized task force" that "could coordinate a single, strategic response" to disinformation. The *Times* may have admitted the idea "sounds a little dystopian," but as a solution to this problem it also sounds nearly as delusional as QAnon. For one thing, how out of touch are the people suggesting this to think that anyone who thinks COVID isn't real, or that the 2020 election was stolen, would ever for 2 seconds believe a government-appointed "reality czar" any more than they believe big tech fact checkers? Also, why on earth would we want a government entity to decide what is and isn't reality? We need far better tools at our disposal in this country than to rely on self-interested entities to mold our reality. We need better critical thinkers, a more thoughtful and aware populace. It won't happen overnight, it'll take time to change consciousness in this way, but it is a far more viable solution than depending on tech giants or the government to decide what is real and what isn't.

The Oxford history professor Yuval Noah Harari, who wrote the famous book *Sapiens: A Brief History of Humankind* (which I actually teach in senior English), inspired me to switch gears on my initial vision for journalism class after I read a *WIRED* article he wrote. Just after making the point that by 2050, thanks to technology, much of what kids learn in schools will be irrelevant, he said,

At present, too many schools focus on cramming information. In the past this made sense, because information was scarce, and even the slow trickle of existing information was repeatedly blocked by censorship...When modern schools came along, teaching every child to read and write and imparting the basic facts of geography, history and biology, they represented an immense improvement.

In contrast, in the twenty-first century we are flooded by enormous amounts of information, and even the censors don't try to block it. Instead, they are busy spreading misinformation or distracting us with irrelevancies. If you live in some provincial Mexican town and you have a smartphone, you can spend many lifetimes just reading Wikipedia, watching TED talks, and taking free online courses. No government can hope to conceal all the information it doesn't like. On the other hand, it is alarmingly easy to inundate the public with conflicting reports and red herrings. People all over the world are but a click away from the latest accounts of the bombardment of Aleppo or of melting ice caps in the Arctic, but there are so many contradictory accounts that it is hard to know what to believe. Besides, countless other things are just a click away, making it difficult to focus, and when politics or science look too complicated it is tempting to switch to funny cat videos, celebrity gossip or porn.

In such a world, the last thing a teacher needs to give her pupils is more information. They already have far too much of it. Instead, people need the ability to make sense of information, to tell the difference between what is important and what is unimportant, and above all to combine many bits of information into a broad picture of the world.

In truth, this has been the ideal of western liberal education for centuries, but up till now even many western schools have been rather slack in fulfilling it. Teachers allowed themselves to focus on shoving data while encouraging pupils "to think for themselves." Due to their fear of authoritarianism, liberal schools had a particular horror of grand narratives. They assumed that as long as we give students lots of data and a modicum of freedom, the students will create their own picture of the world, and even if this generation fails to synthesize all the data into a coherent and meaningful story of the world, there will be plenty of time to construct a good synthesis in the future. We have now run out of time. The decisions we will take in the next few decades will shape the future of life itself, and we can take these decisions based only on our present world view. If this generation lacks a comprehensive view of the cosmos, the future of life will be decided at random.

I had been assigned to teach journalism because I was a former journalist. I had just gotten married the summer before I started teaching and had figured, at least for the first year, I would just model my journalism class after the one I took in high school, which focused on contributing articles and photos about the happenings around school to the school newspaper.

But I got to thinking about how, at a mere 30 years old, in my 8 years out of college I had already worked as a reporter, a painter, in behavioral health, an Ed Tech III, had made money on the side as a musician, an artist, editing a book, and various odd jobs, and now was beginning a new chapter as a teacher. The class I took in high school was tailor-made for me, who had aspired to be a journalist, but my favorite class was in many ways irrelevant for most students. After a semester of hearing from students about how intimidated they were about reading the news and consuming information about the world around them, my new goal was to try my very best to help them make sense of the endless content they are subjected to on a daily basis, and also pass on what I myself have learned about how the world works.

As of 2021, I have seen three groups of seniors graduate high school. These students are faced with similar issues that millennials like myself dealt with: skyrocketing tuition rates and crippling student loan debt, the extreme-likelihood of graduating from college and entering the workforce in the midst of a recession if not full-blown depression due to our capitalist system being completely incapable of handling the test of COVID-19 that other countries passed much more successfully.

And how about the years after their college graduation if

they decide to pursue secondary education? I chuckle to myself thinking back to out-of-touch elders who haplessly suggested I should "get out there and travel" after graduating from college in 2009. With what savings? With what job prospects (we were in the middle of a recession)? When my students enter the workforce post-COVID-19, which will likely make for an interesting situation for working-class people, they will enter a competitive and changing workforce that pays low wages and still come face-to-face with the inevitable pressures (bolstered by social media) of eventually doing adult things like buying a house, starting a family, etc. Even before the effects of COVID were truly felt, a PEW research study indicated that 52 percent of young people (18-29) lived with their parents in September 2020, the highest the rate has been since the Great Depression.

Unless things change they will soon find, just like I did (and this is if they're the lucky ones), they're going to need roommates to afford housing, they're going to be told they deserve low wages until they develop skills in college, and if they go get those skills they'll likely accrue massive debt, they're going to need a partner to buy a house, and they're going to need a chunk of savings to start a family because America still doesn't have universal childcare, universal healthcare, or decent paid leave available even though many poorer countries around the world have such programs in place. To go even further down the line, according to scientific consensus we are in for an impending climate catastrophe that neither the Republican or Democratic Party seem to meaningfully care about. While our politicians disingenuously claim "we can't afford" to do anything about all of these extremely clear problems, the representatives in our "democracy" agree to spend trillions of dollars annually on the military, corporate subsidies, and massive tax breaks for the wealthiest people.

The Right will say it's okay that the 12 richest men in America actually gained one trillion dollars while working families and small business owners suffered during COVID-19 because their wealth will "trickle down" and, besides, people get what they deserve – if you're out of business you didn't work hard enough. They will say we shouldn't tax ultra-wealthy people and entities because they "earned" all of this money not as a product of a rigged system but because they were "innovative" and "work hard." Sure, let's have this conversation. Let's keep both sides in it. I will gladly articulate this other side, and even keep a straight face doing it, but kids aren't stupid, and they actually still have empathy because they haven't yet been beaten over the head in the doldrums of late-stage capitalism or encountered the brain-rot of the right-wing Intellectual Dark Web.

Take another concept that erupted in the summer of 2020: racial tensions. As John Oliver said, "The less you know about history the easier it is to imagine you'd be on the right side of it." And how accurate. It's striking how many adults think that electing a moderate right-wing president who happened to be black erases hundreds of years of brutal history toward black people in which they were bought, sold, bred, and traded like cattle. When we analyze which race dominates economic power currently and see that most is concentrated in the hands of white men, we're forced to consider the reason why – is it because people of color are inferior and lazy or because a handful of white capitalists got a head start while black people not only were not provided with a chance to gain economic power, but were instead literally property? And if the racial component makes you feel uncomfortable because you as a white person have been through tough times as well, I'd say even though those problems didn't arise due to the color of your skin we can still stand in solidarity along the lines of class – and we know indisputably that power, wealth, and influence is increasingly funneled into the hands of a small group of oligarchs in this very country at everyone else's expense. We know undeniably that our government does not work on our behalf despite the fact that the vast majority of the country supports Medicare for All, Green New Deal, and a wealth tax while these bastards claim "we can't afford it" as they write another blank check for militarism, corporate subsidies, and tax breaks for the wealthy. We know for certain, as outlined in painstaking detail in Thomas Picketty's *Capital in the Twenty First Century*, that we're reaching historic levels of inequality that will likely either result in massive poverty or significant social upheaval.

When we are urged to pretend that our country is an infallible masterpiece of democratic goodness and awesomeness, we have no way of ever reckoning with the failures and ongoing problems of our country. When we mindlessly wave American flags and tout ourselves baselessly as the "greatest country on earth" we have descended into Status Quo Warrioring and depressingly submit to the fact that this is as good as it gets. The dishonest right wing will say things like, "we ended slavery so systemic racism isn't a thing" or "how lucky you are to be living the way you are today with your Starbucks and your iPhone." Putting aside the fact that material possessions should probably not be used as a barometer of human well-being, and technological advancements occur with or without capital involved (remember, we landed on the moon and invented the internet not via the magic of the free market, but by using scientific progress, human labor, and tax dollars), you can describe the current situation in juxtaposition with a worse past at any point in history and endlessly argue against progress in this fashion. It's lazy, contemptible, and pathetic, but it's what the Right does and we should not be afraid to call it out in public schools, places of *education* where the *truth* should prevail.

Progress shouldn't be politicized. Improving material conditions for more people shouldn't be politicized. These should be foregone conclusions and aspirations as a society, and lessons for our youth, but the Right by nature seeks not to improve anything for the masses, but instead to preserve the status quo and maintain power within the private sector since that's where power currently heavily lies in America. The Left wants a floor for people to stand on, the Right wants to stand on these people, all the while convincing them the wealth will trickle down. On one hand we have the concept of healthcare, childcare, or even college being held in public hands, on the other we have paying exorbitant costs so a handful of people can make a profit. The one kid who wants to be a healthcare insurance CEO and profit from cancer patients so he can buy a yacht will relate to the Right (but will his dream actually come true?), the rest will likely want cheaper healthcare, education, childcare costs, maybe an economic situation that leaves them in a position to move out of their parents' house and purchase a home. We know the existing reality, we know the problems that exist. Not teaching this stuff at all preserves the status quo and leaves people behind. Teaching both sides leaves kids with a decision to support left or right-wing economics and law and order proposals. The concept of merely addressing these issues en masse is scary for the powerful because the Left's mission is enticing to the masses, the Right's is great for a handful of people already in power. If both are described honestly, it's a no-brainer.

Of course, at times the gaslighting takes its toll on me. I post about this stuff on social media, I write articles for my paper, and I take on all feedback, I don't unfriend or block people. I always keep the possibility in the back of my mind that I might be wrong about my beliefs in dealing with the existing problems in this country. But what I would do personally isn't really what is discussed in class. We discuss homelessness. We discuss wealth inequality. We discuss corruption in the political system. We discuss the climate crisis, the criminal justice system, economics, and a host of other issues. We discuss the intricacies of journalism and the consumption of information and education as a vital component to a functioning democracy. We talk about very real issues that plague our country instead of pretending everything is perfect the way it is, or focusing on what I consider to be less-substantial topics, and we discuss how we might solve these issues. Frankly, though I am quite happy with my personal life, I feel very deeply for others. There are plenty of things that would help my cause (universal healthcare and childcare as I start my own family for example) but I think I am lucky enough to be in a position that my wife and I will be able to grind by. But I find it a lot more inspiring to imagine a better world for others who aren't so lucky. I find it more humane to discuss the possibilities of a better world rather than shame anyone who hasn't made it into thinking they are just a failure who didn't work hard enough, and somehow failed to make a success out of themselves in this supposed "land of opportunity." When we actually operate on the basis that anyone can be wealthy and successful if they just put their mind to it, and blame anyone who isn't wealthy, successful, and comfortable on their own personal failings rather than look at big, powerful systems holding people back, is it any wonder people become depressed in a late-stage capitalist society? Is it any wonder younger generations are depressed, or marriages fail, or suicide rates rise?

Teachers don't know everything. At the very least we should get kids to understand our world is incredibly complicated and we should be open to hearing different points of view. Frankly, when you stack up Michael Brooks vs. Dave Rubin, Briahna Joy Gray vs. Ben Shapiro, Cornel West vs. Sam Harris, Richard Wolff vs. Dennis Prager, or anyone from Chapo Trap House vs. Jordan Peterson, the more factual, logical, and moral ideology is absurdly obvious. To be very clear: giving both sides of the argument, at least if done well and in fairness, is advantageous for the Left and the working class. Not discussing these matters at all and allowing ahistorical grifters to fill the voids of curiosity is advantageous to a handful of people on the Right and already in power, the grifters included. The "Intellectual Dark Web" has no answer for actual leftist intellectuals; which is precisely why they ignore worthy opponents and opt to pick on much easier targets, such as made-up strawman arguments or young college students, to pretend like they are so dominant. Earnestly juxtapose legitimate leftists voices with the faux-intellectuals of the Right and it's not hard to see who has a better handle on history, who has more humane morals, and who cares more about facts than (racist, classist) feelings. With any luck I'll have written this book well enough to be off their radar of easy targets to debate and "destroy." They don't tackle difficult opponents because *it's too difficult and it might become clear that they are wrong*. People generally aren't against actual left-leaning public policy if described honestly, they're against distorted strawman versions of policies mischaracterized both by right-wing "intellectuals," corporate media, and even moderate right wingers like Obama. Whether or not it is intentional, right-wing grifters are masters at inoculation theory – they present bastardized versions of "left" arguments, "destroy" them, and disingenuously claim victory without even having had an honest discussion. They dishonestly describe the corporatism of the Democratic Party as "Marxist" or "leftist," and thereby bury what working-class politics actually mean. For this reason, schools should discuss these issues in depth early and often.

Matt Christman of the podcast Chapo Trap House got me teary-eyed (which is weird, because the show is generally humorous) with a quote in early 2020 just before Bernie Sanders lost to the establishment in the primaries:

> We're not in the worst physical circumstances but everything feels hollow, cynical, and empty. I really do think one of the big reasons for that is because we all know deep down inside there's something wrong with this country, with this world,

with this fucking social order. We know deep down that no humane society would be ordered this way...If good people of good faith, like the people you know in your lives, created a society they wouldn't make this one.

But that knowledge sits right next to the messages we get every day from our parents, our bosses, our media, that this devil's bargain that we've struck where you get creature comfort and convenience in exchange for precarity, alienation, despair, and the steady erosion of the living environment we need to survive, is a choice we made and we opted for this option.

But we know in our hearts that's not true, we know that we never asked for this, that we never wanted this. But the problem is that we're all fucking powerless against it. As an individual what are you supposed to do? Against these massive, world-spanning powers that determine the world that you live in? And so you're left in this position of being hyper-aware of the awfulness and the rot of the world around you coupled with the complete and hyper-specific knowledge of your own inability to do anything about it. And what it does over time is that it starts to eat away at you. And honestly, speaking for myself anyway, it makes you start to hate yourself a little bit. You hate yourself for how powerless you are. And more importantly and more insidiously than that, you start to feel complicit in your own misery. You start to feel complicity in the misery of others. You start to blame yourself because – why aren't you doing anything? But what's to be done?

This campaign, the Bernie Sanders campaign, I swear to God you guys, this is the first movement that any of us have seen in our living lives that has the promise of bringing a mass, a critical mass of people to the realization that they aren't alone. That there is such a thing as a common dream of a more humane world that we can fucking make. But it's because, yes, none of us by ourselves can do anything. That's what they tell you every day to keep you where you are. But what the Bernie campaign is telling you, and what we're all telling ourselves, what we're all telling each other, what all you canvassers are saying, what people are saying at dinner tables, what people are talking about, what people are saying more and more is that all of us together can do anything.

I keep a David Graeber quote on my classroom wall, "The ultimate hidden truth of the world is that it is something we make and could as easily make differently." Though the Sanders campaign has come and gone, together we can still do a great deal, with education we can make strives if not for ourselves for future generations. We owe it to our kids and their kid's kids to discuss the issues referenced in these pages and much more in public schools, we owe it to them to fight for a better future, and I owe it to them as a teacher to be a lifelong learner who is going to continue to pass along my findings to them. With right-wing leaders and governments cropping up throughout the world, who are experts at dishonestly channeling rage by pointing their fingers not at the powers that be but at "illegals," "freeloaders on welfare," "Muslims," and other easy, voiceless targets, we need an entity to set the record straight early on. In America, our current alternative to right-wing law and order neofascism is a right-of-center Democratic Party that sooner engages in platitudes and symbolic gestures than realistic policy reform. We shouldn't allow these two parties to be able to pander to ignorant voters on such useless drivel, we should educate future generations and arm them with the tools to spot bullshit when they see it not only in politics, but in their future workplace or information consumption. We should lift them up and illustrate a better world is possible rather than pretend like this is as good as it could possibly get.

To start each second semester, I check in on my students to

find out if their confidence in media consumption is improving at all. An incredibly bright student of mine said early in 2021, though she felt more comfortable finding sources to trust and found it interesting to know what was happening in the world, she ultimately felt absolutely powerless in doing anything about the issues that plague this country.

"All I can do about any of this is read the news, get angry, and cast a vote," she said, and described wondering why she should even bother knowing what is going on in the world at all. I asked the rest of the class if they felt a similar way, and about 15 hands went up. It was one of those moments as a teacher where the lesson plan goes out the window because the students themselves brought up a more important matter to address.

I told them there is far more you can do than simply vote to help change the world, or make the country a better place. Contrary to what Barack Obama and other faux-progressives will have you believe, going and checking a box every 2-4 years isn't the only game in town. I couldn't have been more disappointed when Obama met with LeBron James when NBA players were flirting with a strike. He may not have told him to "shut up and dribble," but more or less said "shut up, dribble, and vote" instead of meaningful activism that would have undoubtedly garnered attention. There is a world of other approaches to take in making positive change in this world aside from voting. Get educated on the issues, become an activist, run for local office, become a lawyer, become a teacher. Unionize your workplace. Work for the Sunrise Movement or a similar social justice group. Become an investigative journalist. Build coalitions, have conversations, educate others, organize, and protest. Any change that may come isn't going to happen overnight, it's going to take a long struggle. I told them if they were up to the challenge mentally, because you can't focus on the big issues if your own mental health is struggling, then get out there and dedicate your energy into making the world a better place. I was proud and inspired when they seemed to understand there was a hell of a lot more to meaningful social change than simply casting a vote.

I remain humble, and I haven't ruled out that perhaps I am only saying this because I happened to stumble into education, but it seems to me that there is a battle of information afoot, and the good side of this battle must be led by public schools and on behalf of the masses. The journalist in me says my role is still to help inform people, so now instead of writing for a paper, I teach in a classroom. Whether you're a teacher who decides to use my journalism curriculum verbatim, or an educator who has been inspired to incorporate some of these ideas in your existing curriculum, or just a parent or citizen who read this book and began thinking more deeply about information, propaganda, media consumption, and US politics, I thank you from the bottom of my heart and am glad to have you on the right side of history, the quest for making a better world. Humanity needs people like us to acknowledge our shared humanity, stick together, build, and make things happen now more than ever.

Here is a reading and content list that brought me to where I am at. This is everything I can think of that I read through the years that may have shaped my thinking in writing this book and making this curriculum. I am sure I am forgetting some, others I've left off intentionally that weren't quite as impactful for me. Some I have already mentioned in this book and use in class, others I consumed and they naturally contributed to my world experience thus affecting my bias. This list is added to constantly:

Hate Inc. – Matt Taibbi – an updated critique on media
Manufacturing Consent – Edward Herman and Noam Chomsky
    – the classic OG critique of media.
Dirty Wars – Jeremy Scahill – US foreign policy.
Power Systems
Failed States
Global Discontents
Hegemony or Survival
Imperial Ambitions
Consequences of Capitalism
Chomsky for Activists – all by Noam Chomsky – US foreign policy
    and general inner workings of the world.
America's Real Business in Iraq
The Shock Doctrine
No Is Not Enough
This Changes Everything
On Fire – all by Naomi Klein generally dealing with the climate
    crisis and disaster capitalism.
Amusing Ourselves to Death – Neil Postman – a 1985 book
    critiquing television, but a lot of what he says can be applied
    to the internet.
Republic of Lies – Ana Merlan – a deep dive into conspiracy
    theories.
The People's Platform

Democracy May Not Exist, But We'll Miss It When It's Gone – both by Astra Taylor – a great look into the importance of democracy – and she also made a documentary about it.

Democracy at Work – Richard Wolff – wonderful ideas for democratizing American workplaces and moving America leftward.

Chaos – Tom O'Neil – an unbelievable look at the Manson murders and how the intelligence community fights left ideas domestically.

Capital in the Twenty-First Century – Thomas Picketty – a thorough look at how wealth inequality is becoming increasingly unsustainable.

Listen Liberal

What's the Matter With Kansas

Rendezvous with Oblivion

Pity the Billionaire – all by Thomas Frank – four great books hammering both political parties and also far-right economic policy.

Utopia for Realists – Rutger Bregman

Why You Should Be a Socialist – Nathan Robinson

The ABCs of Socialism – Jacobin Magazine – These three books are inspiring solutions to many of the problems we encounter today. A lot more positive and uplifting than other selections on this list.

Canceling Comedians While the World Burns

Give Them an Argument – both by Ben Burgis – a critique of the reactionary Left and discussion on logic for leftist arguments.

Don't Think of an Elephant – George Lakoff – discussion on forming arguments and framing.

Economics in One Lesson – Henry Hazlitt – a favorite for right wingers, a book that sheds light on why right wingers think the way they do. I wrote a piece about it in my local paper, the *Kennebec Journal*, you may be able to Google.

Das Kapital

The Communist Manifesto – Karl Marx

American Fascists

America: The Farewell Tour – Chris Hedges – In-depth looks at the American religious right and the startling erosion of this country.

How Fascism Works – Jason Stanley – it's alarming how much historical examples of fascism mirror US politics.

How Propaganda Works – another Jason Stanley book, and ultimately, I believe, a more thorough, articulate, and philosophical case for curriculums like mine.

Why We're Polarized – Ezra Klein

A People's History of the United States – Howard Zinn – a left-leaning version of American history in that it puts working people as the focus of success.

A Patriot's History of the United States – Larry Schwiekart and Michael Allen – a right-leaning version of American history in that it puts business and economics as the focus of success. Go ahead and read and compare the two.

Saving Capitalism

The Common Good – Robert Reich – a look at economics from a moderate economist.

Enlightenment Now – Steven Pinker – a moderate glance at the world that highlights many advancements and improvements, but notably omits or marginalizes many problems, most obviously the climate crisis.

Propaganda – Edward Bernays – the father of public relations speaks out.

The Righteous Mind – Jonathan Haidt – a look at why Americans continue to polarize.

Super Thinking – *Gabriel Weinberg and Lauren McCann*

The Skeptics Guide to the Universe – Steven Novella

You Are Not So Smart – David McRaney – three solid books on critical thinking, conspiracy theories, and general skepticism of information.

How To Be Anti-Racist – Ibram X. Kendi

The New Jim Crow – Michelle Alexander – a look at mass incarceration and colorblindness in America.

One Person, No Vote – Carol Anderson – well-researched historic look at the political process keeping people from voting.

On the Clock – Emily Guendelsberger – an undercover journalist works at McDonalds, Amazon, and call centers and tells about her experience.

Bull Shit Jobs – David Graeber – Graeber estimates 50 percent of jobs are completely unnecessary. Might be time to reevaluate.

Falter – Bill McKibben

Sapiens

21 Lessons for the 21st Century – Yuval Noah Harari

The Cost of Loyalty – Tim Bakken – a look at the hubris in the US military.

Full Dissidence – Howard Bryant – a collection of hard-hitting essays by sportswriter Bryant about race relations and other issues of the day.

Breaking Through Power – Ralph Nader

Guns, Germs, and Steel – Jared Diamond – a broad look at human history.

The Creature from Jekyll Island – G. Edward Griffin – a libertarian look at the banking system.

Weekly/Daily Podcasts:

Citations Needed – a great media criticism podcast that tackles all kinds of media tropes – basically a deep dive into manufactured consent on an array of issues.

Useful Idiots – a podcast by journalists Matt Taibbi and Katie Halper.

Intercepted – a podcast by Jeremy Scahill, founder of The Intercept.

Chapo Trap House – a humorous yet informative leftist podcast.

Economic Update – a weekly podcast by Marxist economist

Richard Wolff.

Bad Faith – Briahna Joy Gray and Chapo's Virgil Texas host excellent panels of guests.

The Tightrope – Cornel West and Tricia Rose's philosophical and political podcast.

Sources (that hold both parties accountable!):

The Intercept

Jacobin

The Nation

The Daily Poster

Current Affairs

Democracy Now!

CULTURE, SOCIETY & POLITICS

Contemporary culture has eliminated the concept and public figure of the intellectual. A cretinous anti-intellectualism presides, cheer-led by hacks in the pay of multinational corporations who reassure their bored readers that there is no need to rouse themselves from their stupor. Zer0 Books knows that another kind of discourse - intellectual without being academic, popular without being populist - is not only possible: it is already flourishing. Zer0 is convinced that in the unthinking, blandly consensual culture in which we live, critical and engaged theoretical reflection is more important than ever before.

If you have enjoyed this book, why not tell other readers by posting a review on your preferred book site.

You may also wish to
subscribe to our Zer0 Books YouTube Channel.

Bestsellers from Zer0 Books include:

Give Them An Argument
Logic for the Left
Ben Burgis
Many serious leftists have learned to distrust talk of logic. This is
a serious mistake.
Paperback: 978-1-78904-210-8 ebook: 978-1-78904-211-5

Poor but Sexy
Culture Clashes in Europe East and West
Agata Pyzik
How the East stayed East and the West stayed West.
Paperback: 978-1-78099-394-2 ebook: 978-1-78099-395-9

An Anthropology of Nothing in Particular
Martin Demant Frederiksen
A journey into the social lives of meaninglessness.
Paperback: 978-1-78535-699-5 ebook: 978-1-78535-700-8

In the Dust of This Planet
Horror of Philosophy vol. 1
Eugene Thacker
In the first of a series of three books on the Horror of Philosophy,
In the Dust of This Planet offers the genre of horror as a way of
thinking about the unthinkable.
Paperback: 978-1-84694-676-9 ebook: 978-1-78099-010-1

The End of Oulipo?
An Attempt to Exhaust a Movement
Lauren Elkin, Veronica Esposito
Paperback: 978-1-78099-655-4 ebook: 978-1-78099-656-1

Capitalist Realism

Is There No Alternative?

Mark Fisher

An analysis of the ways in which capitalism has presented itself
as the only realistic political-economic system.

Paperback: 978-1-84694-317-1 ebook: 978-1-78099-734-6

Rebel Rebel

Chris O'Leary

David Bowie: every single song. Everything you want to know,
everything you didn't know.

Paperback: 978-1-78099-244-0 ebook: 978-1-78099-713-1

Kill All Normies

Angela Nagle

Online culture wars from 4chan and Tumblr to Trump.

Paperback: 978-1-78535-543-1 ebook: 978-1-78535-544-8

Cartographies of the Absolute

Alberto Toscano, Jeff Kinkle

An aesthetics of the economy for the twenty-first century.

Paperback: 978-1-78099-275-4 ebook: 978-1-78279-973-3

Malign Velocities

Accelerationism and Capitalism

Benjamin Noys

Long listed for the Bread and Roses Prize 2015, *Malign Velocities*
argues against the need for speed, tracking acceleration
as the symptom of the ongoing crises of capitalism.

Paperback: 978-1-78279-300-7 ebook: 978-1-78279-299-4

Meat Market
Female Flesh under Capitalism
Laurie Penny
A feminist dissection of women's bodies as the fleshy fulcrum of
capitalist cannibalism, whereby women are both consumers and
consumed.

Paperback: 978-1-84694-521-2 ebook: 978-1-84694-782-7

Babbling Corpse
Vaporwave and the Commodification of Ghosts
Grafton Tanner

Paperback: 978-1-78279-759-3 ebook: 978-1-78279-760-9

New Work New Culture
Work we want and a culture that strengthens us
Frithjof Bergmann
A serious alternative for mankind and the planet.

Paperback: 978-1-78904-064-7 ebook: 978-1-78904-065-4

Romeo and Juliet in Palestine
Teaching Under Occupation
Tom Sperlinger
Life in the West Bank, the nature of pedagogy and the role of a
university under occupation.

Paperback: 978-1-78279-637-4 ebook: 978-1-78279-636-7

Color, Facture, Art and Design
Iona Singh
This materialist definition of fine-art develops guidelines for
architecture, design, cultural-studies and ultimately social
change.

Paperback: 978-1-78099-629-5 ebook: 978-1-78099-630-1

Sweetening the Pill
or How We Got Hooked on Hormonal Birth Control
Holly Grigg-Spall
Has contraception liberated or oppressed women?
Sweetening the Pill breaks the silence on the dark side of hormonal
contraception.
Paperback: 978-1-78099-607-3 ebook: 978-1-78099-608-0

Why Are We The Good Guys?
Reclaiming Your Mind from the Delusions of Propaganda
David Cromwell
A provocative challenge to the standard ideology that Western
power is a benevolent force in the world.
Paperback: 978-1-78099-365-2 ebook: 978-1-78099-366-9

The Writing on the Wall
On the Decomposition of Capitalism and its Critics
Anselm Jappe, Alastair Hemmens
A new approach to the meaning of social emancipation.
Paperback: 978-1-78535-581-3 ebook: 978-1-78535-582-0

Enjoying It
Candy Crush and Capitalism
Alfie Bown
A study of enjoyment and of the enjoyment of studying. Bown
asks what enjoyment says about us and what we say about
enjoyment, and why.
Paperback: 978-1-78535-155-6 ebook: 978-1-78535-156-3

Ghosts of My Life
Writings on Depression, Hauntology and Lost Futures
Mark Fisher
Paperback: 978-1-78099-226-6 ebook: 978-1-78279-624-4

Neglected or Misunderstood
The Radical Feminism of Shulamith Firestone
Victoria Margree
An interrogation of issues surrounding gender, biology,
sexuality, work and technology, and the ways in which our
imaginations continue to be in thrall to ideologies of maternity
and the nuclear family.
Paperback: 978-1-78535-539-4 ebook: 978-1-78535-540-0

How to Dismantle the NHS in 10 Easy Steps (Second Edition)
Youssef El-Gingihy
The story of how your NHS was sold off and why you will have
to buy private health insurance soon. A new expanded second
edition with chapters on junior doctors' strikes and government
blueprints for US-style healthcare.
Paperback: 978-1-78904-178-1 ebook: 978-1-78904-179-8

Digesting Recipes
The Art of Culinary Notation
Susannah Worth
A recipe is an instruction, the imperative tone of the expert, but
this constraint can offer its own kind of potential. A recipe need
not be a domestic trap but might instead offer escape – something
to fantasise about or aspire to.
Paperback: 978-1-78279-860-6 ebook: 978-1-78279-859-0

Most titles are published in paperback and as an ebook.
Paperbacks are available in traditional bookshops. Both print and
ebook formats are available online.
Follow us at:
https://www.facebook.com/ZeroBooks
https://twitter.com/Zer0Books
https://www.instagram.com/zero.books